Other titles include *Up & Running* with:

AutoSketch 3

Carbon Copy Plus

Clipper 5.01

CorelDRAW 2

dBASE III PLUS

DOS 3.3

DOS 5

DR DOS 5.0

Excel 3 for Windows

Flight Simulator

Grammatik IV 2.0

Harvard Graphics

Harvard Graphics 3

Lotus 1-2-3 Release 2.2

Lotus 1-2-3 Release 2.3

Lotus 1-2-3 Release 3.1

Mac Classic

Mac System 7

Norton Desktop for
 Windows

Norton Utilities

Norton Utilities 5

Norton Utilities on the
 Macintosh

PageMaker 4 on the PC

PageMaker on the Macintosh

PC Tools Deluxe 6

PC-Write

PROCOMM PLUS

PROCOMM PLUS 2.0

Q & A

Q & A 4

Quattro Pro 3

Quicken 4

ToolBook for Windows

Turbo Pascal 5.5

Windows 3.0

Windows 286/386

Word for Windows

WordPerfect 5.1

WordPerfect
 Library/Office PC

XTreeGold 2

Your Hard Disk

Computer users are not all alike.
Neither are SYBEX books.

We know our customers have a variety of needs. They've told us so. And because we've listened, we've developed several distinct types of books to meet the needs of each of our customers. What are you looking for in computer help?

If you're looking for the basics, try the **ABC's** series, or for a more visual approach, select **Teach Yourself.**

Mastering and **Understanding** titles offer you a step-by-step introduction, plus an in-depth examination of intermediate-level features, to use as you progress.

Our **Up & Running** series is designed for computer-literate consumers who want a no-nonsense overview of new programs. Just 20 basic lessons, and you're on your way.

SYBEX **Encyclopedias** and **Desktop References** provide a comprehensive reference and explanation of all of the commands, features and functions of the subject software.

Sometimes a subject requires a special treatment that our standard series don't provide. So you'll find we have titles like **Advanced Techniques, Handbooks, Tips & Tricks,** and others that are specifically tailored to satisfy a unique need.

You'll find SYBEX publishes a variety of books on every popular software package. Looking for computer help? Help Yourself to SYBEX.

For a complete catalog of our publications:

SYBEX Inc.
2021 Challenger Drive, Alameda, CA 94501
Tel: (510) 523-8233/(800) 227-2346 Telex: 336311
Fax: (510) 523-2373

Up & Running with
Lotus 1-2-3®for Windows™

Robert M. Thomas

SYBEX®

San Francisco • Paris • Düsseldorf • Soest

Acquisitions Editor: David J. Clark
Series Editor: Joanne Cuthbertson
Editor: David Krassner
Technical Editors: Nick Dargahi and Michael Gross
Word Processors: Ann Dunn and Susan Trybull
Book Designer: Elke Hermanowski
Icon Designer: Helen Bruno
Screen Graphics: Cuong Le
Desktop Production Artist: Claudia Smelser
Proofreaders: Catherine Mahoney and Janet Boone
Indexer: Robert M. Thomas
Cover Designer: Archer Design

Library of Congress Card Number: 91-75248
ISBN: 0-89588-873-4

Manufactured in the United States of America
10 9 8 7 6 5 4 3 2 1

SYBEX
Up & Running Books

The Up & Running series of books from SYBEX has been developed for committed, eager PC users who would like to become familiar with a wide variety of programs and operations as quickly as possible. We assume that you are comfortable with your PC and that you know the basic functions of word processing, spreadsheets, and database management. With this background, Up & Running books will show you in 20 steps what particular products can do and how to use them.

Up & Running books are designed to save you time and money. First, you can avoid purchase mistakes by previewing products before you buy them—exploring their features, strengths, and limitations. Second, once you decide to purchase a product, you can learn its basics quickly by following the 20 steps—even if you are a beginner.

The first step usually covers software installation in relation to hardware requirements. You'll learn whether the program can operate with your available hardware as well as various methods for starting the program. The second step often introduces the program's user interface. The remaining 18 steps demonstrate the program's basic functions, using examples and short descriptions.

A clock shows the amount of time you can expect to spend at your computer for each step. Naturally, you'll need much less time if you only read through the step rather than complete it at your computer.

You can also focus on particular points by scanning the short notes in the margins and locating the sections you are most interested in.

In addition, three symbols highlight particular sections of text:

 The Action symbol highlights important steps that you will carry out.

 The Tip symbol indicates a practical hint or special technique.

 The Warning symbol alerts you to a potential problem and suggestions for avoiding it.

We have structured the Up & Running books so that the busy user spends little time studying documentation and is not burdened with unnecessary text. An Up & Running book cannot, of course, replace a lengthier book that contains advanced applications. However, you will get the information you need to put the program to practical use and to learn its basic functions in the shortest possible time.

We welcome your comments

SYBEX is very interested in your reactions to the Up & Running series. Your opinions and suggestions will help all of our readers, including yourself. Please send your comments to: SYBEX Editorial Department, 2021 Challenger Drive, Alameda, CA 94501.

Preface

Lotus 1-2-3 takes a time-honored business tool—the accountant's spreadsheet—gives it increased power and flexibility, and places it in the memory of a desktop computer. Since its introduction in 1983, 1-2-3 has grown to become one of the world's most widely used business computer applications. Today it is used by more than five million people.

This book covers the basic features of 1-2-3 for Windows. Whether you are a brand-new user of Lotus 1-2-3, or just a busy person who needs a quick understanding of the product's capabilities, this book is for you. It will introduce you to the fundamentals of 1-2-3, give you an overview of its capabilities, and show you how to be as productive as possible. When you complete the steps in this book, you will be able to create and format useful spreadsheets, use them to produce graphs, store and manipulate information in a database, and enhance the appearance of your printouts with 1-2-3's worksheet-formatting features.

Should you wish to learn more about 1-2-3's advanced features, the information you acquire in this book will provide you with a solid foundation for additional learning, giving you the confidence to experiment freely and helping you better understand 1-2-3's documentation.

If you have just purchased a copy of Lotus 1-2-3 but have not yet installed it or used it, read the first two steps carefully. They will tell you how to set up the software on your computer and show you how to navigate 1-2-3's menu system. The remaining steps should be read in order, because many of the later steps assume an understanding of information presented in earlier ones. The time required to complete each step is indicated at the beginning, so that you can budget your learning time.

This book assumes that you are already familiar with the Microsoft Windows 3.0 commands and interface, to the extent that you can run programs and are familiar with Windows' menu and dialog-box conventions. Lotus 1-2-3 for Windows is fully integrated into the Microsoft Windows 3.0 operating environment and makes liberal use of Windows' standard features. If you are new to Windows, take some time to learn that program before attempting to learn 1-2-3 for Windows.

If you have used 1-2-3 for DOS, you can make use of a special menu of old-style 1-2-3 commands called "1-2-3 Classic," which will appear when you press the forward slash key in 1-2-3's READY mode. This book assumes that, whether you are a new 1-2-3 user or experienced in the DOS version, you are interested in learning to use the Windows interface, rather than relying on the old command style. If you are a new user and are interested in learning the DOS menu commands, pick up a copy of *Up & Running with Lotus 1-2-3 Release 3.1* for details.

The keys to becoming an expert at Lotus 1-2-3 are understanding the software and practicing. This book provides that understanding; the practice is up to you. Enjoy learning the program.

Table of Contents

Step 1

Installation

Step 1 describes the system requirements for Lotus 1-2-3 for Windows, outlining how you must prepare the software to run it on your system. You will be guided through 1-2-3's basic installation procedure and you will learn how to start 1-2-3 from within Windows.

1-2-3's System Requirements

Before you purchase 1-2-3 for Windows, be sure that your system can run the program. If you are uncertain of any of the technical requirements below, consult with your dealer.

1-2-3 for Windows requires the following:

- An IBM PC (or fully compatible), using an 80286, 80386, or 80486 CPU, that can run Microsoft Windows Version 3.0 or later, under DOS version 3.11 or later. (Microsoft recommends using DOS Version 5.0 to run Windows 3.0, because of its enhanced memory-management features.)

- A minimum of 2 Mb of random-access memory (RAM), with 4 Mb or more preferred. If you are running Windows in Standard Mode, it is possible to run 1-2-3 for Windows in as little as 1 Mb of RAM, but software performance is significantly hampered when using this little RAM.

- A hard disk. If you are planning to install all of 1-2-3's included add-in programs and tutorial files, you will need at least 6 Mb of available space for the program files, plus extra room for the data files you will create.

- One floppy-disk drive, either 3• inch or 5• inch, for loading the software files.

- A monitor with graphics capability. 1-2-3 for Windows will work with any Windows-compatible monitor. You'll probably want a monitor with an EGA or a VGA card if you plan to work with graphs and enhanced worksheet text.

The following equipment, although not strictly required, extends the range of things you can do with 1-2-3 for Windows:

- To produce hard copies of worksheets, you need a printer. The printer should have good graphics capabilities for producing hard copy of your graphs and enhanced worksheets.

- To move more easily around the worksheet, menus, and windows without resorting to keyboard commands, you need a *mouse*.

Installing the Program

Installing tells 1-2-3 what hardware you use

Before installing 1-2-3, make working copies of the master disks. The master disks are too valuable to be used for any purpose other than making working copies for your own use. Use the DOS DISKCOPY command to make these working copies, then store the master disks in a secure location. If you aren't sure how to use DISKCOPY, refer to your DOS documentation.

Use the working copies to install the software on your system. To begin the installation procedure, do as follows:

1. Start Windows and open the Program Manager.

2. Place the disk labeled *Install* in your computer's floppy-disk drive.

3. Pick File from the Menu Bar, followed by **Run**.

4. In the Command Line box, type

   A:INSTALL.EXE

   If the disk drive containing the install disk is not A, substitute your drive letter and a colon for *A:* in the above example.

5. Pick the OK button (or press Enter).

The installation procedure, though time-consuming, is easy to follow. You will be presented with a series of dialog boxes similar to
those found in standard Windows applications. Read each dialog box
carefully; if you wish to proceed with the installation, pick the OK
button (or press Enter). Most dialog boxes also include Help and
Cancel buttons.

If you do not have a mouse, you can pick a button by holding down
the keyboard's Alt key and pressing the letter that is underlined in the
button's label. There will always be one button highlighted. You can
highlight other available buttons by pressing the arrow keys. To pick
a highlighted button, press Enter.

The first time you run the installation program, 1-2-3 will ask you to
initialize the System Disk with your name and the name of your
business. Enter this information carefully. It is recorded permanently
on your install disk as well as in the installed program on your hard
disk and cannot be changed afterward.

The main installation menu, pictured in Figure 1.1, offers the
following options. Select the desired option by picking its corre-
sponding button:

- Install 1-2-3

- View Product Updates

- Choose International Options

  For now, just pick the Install 1-2-3 button. 1-2-3 presents
  you with two options:

- *Install with Defaults*, which will install a standard configuration of 1-2-3 on your hard disk

- *Install with Options*, which allows advanced users to
  choose various configuration options

If you are a new user, pick *Install with Defaults*.

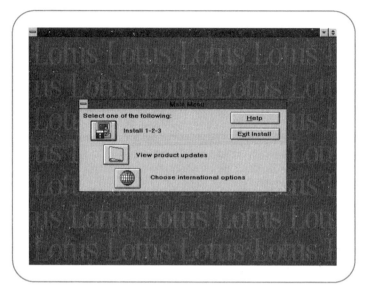

Figure 1.1: The main installation menu

If you pick *Install with Options*, you can elect to transfer the 1-2-3 system files, the Translate Utility, or sample worksheets to your hard disk. You can also choose the DataLens drivers for displaying data in other file formats within a 1-2-3 worksheet.

1-2-3 prompts you to specify the drive and subdirectory name on which you intend to install the program, offering *C:\123W* as the default. In addition, 1-2-3 displays the amount of available space on each of your system's disk drives, the amount of disk space required by the configuration you have chosen, and the amount of space that will remain on the drive after installation.

You can change the drive and directory defaults by picking the indicated text box and entering the desired drive letter or subdirectory name. If you enter a subdirectory name that contains files, 1-2-3 will prompt you to confirm that you want to overwrite files.

The installation's progress is monitored on the screen, keeping you informed about how much of the process is complete. A Cancel button is always available on screen, allowing you to abort the process at any time.

When the installation is finished, 1-2-3 returns to the Install Main Menu, where you can pick another option, get help, or exit to Windows by picking the appropriate button. When you exit, you will notice that the install program has created a new program window named *Lotus Applications*. This window contains two icons: one for Lotus 1-2-3, and the other for the Lotus Installation Program. You can move these icons or make any desired changes to the program window using standard Windows commands.

1-2-3 reads your Windows configuration for information about your display type. If you change display types at a later time, update your Windows configuration and 1-2-3 will update automatically to reflect the change. Printer setup will be discussed in Step 13, *Printing Spreadsheets.*

Starting Lotus 1-2-3

Once you have indicated your hardware equipment, you are ready to start 1-2-3. Enter Windows and pick the *1-2-3 for Windows* icon.

Step 2

User Interface

This step describes the structure of a 1-2-3 worksheet and explains the elements in the screen display. It also shows you how to move around the spreadsheet and how to use special keys to manipulate the worksheet with maximum efficiency.

Whenever you start the program, the screen displays a *worksheet,* the grid of rows and columns where you will enter text and numbers, plus formulas and functions for calculating meaningful relationships among the items you enter. The opening worksheet is illustrated in Figure 2.1.

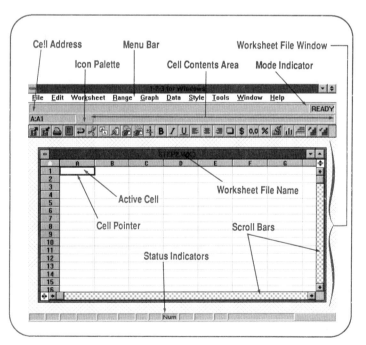

Figure 2.1: The opening worksheet display

Rows, Columns, and Cells

A basic 1-2-3 worksheet consists of numbered horizontal *rows*, which are divided into lettered vertical *columns*. In addition, the worksheet file may contain as many as 256 worksheet *layers*. Each layer can have up to 8192 rows and 256 columns.

These rows and columns are not all visible on the screen at the same time. Instead, the screen operates as a movable window into the spreadsheet, displaying only a small portion of it.

Rows in 1-2-3 are numbered sequentially from 1 to 8,192. Columns are identified using letters, running from *A* to *Z*, then *AA* to *AZ*, *BA* to *BZ*, and so on to column *IV*. Worksheet layers are also identified with letters, starting with *A* and continuing through *IV*.

The intersection of a row and column on a layer is called a *cell*. A worksheet's data is entered into its cells. Each cell has a unique *cell address*, consisting of its layer ID (if more than one worksheet layer is being used), followed by its column ID, followed by its row number. Thus, the cell in the upper-leftmost corner of the first layer of the worksheet has the address A:A1, and the cell in the lower-rightmost corner has the address A:IV8192. The same cells on worksheet layer B would have the addresses B:A1 and B:IV8192. If you have enough memory and disk storage space, you can have up to 536,870,912 cells in a single worksheet file.

At any given time, at least one cell is *active*, meaning that you may enter data into this cell from the keyboard or manipulate its contents. The active cell is indicated by the *cell pointer*, a highlighted box that can be moved about the worksheet with the arrow keys or mouse. In addition, the address of the active cell is always shown in the upper-left corner of the worksheet's window.

A range *is a group of adjacent cells*

Certain commands can operate on a group of adjacent cells, called a *range*. You define a range by specifying the cell addresses of two opposite corners, usually the upper-left and lower-right, called the *starting cell* and *ending cell* of the range. A range can include cells on adjacent layers.

The basic technique for defining a range is simple: first move the cell pointer to one corner of the range, then hold down the mouse's pick button and move the cell pointer to the opposite corner of the range. If you are using the keyboard, press the F4 function key after highlighting the starting cell, then move the cell pointer to the opposite corner of the range using the keyboard's arrow keys.

The 1-2-3 Screen

Whenever you start 1-2-3, you will see the opening worksheet display. The components of this display are labeled in Figure 2.1, and they are described in the sections that follow.

Menu Bar

The *Menu Bar* appears near the top of the screen, and contains a list of keywords that open other *pull-down menus*, which contain various 1-2-3 commands. For example, one of the most important commands to know is the one that saves your work to disk. To save the current worksheet data, pick the File keyword from the menu bar, followed by the Save command from the pull-down menu. You can accomplish the same thing using the keyboard by pressing Alt-FS. (Please note: When I say something like "press Alt-FS," I mean "press Alt-F and then press S.")

The menu bar contains 1-2-3's commands

Some menu commands open *dialog boxes*, as shown in Figure 2.2. Once open, dialog boxes can be moved around the screen like any other window, allowing you greater flexibility in seeing portions of the worksheet file, or multiple dialog boxes, while considering and selecting options.

To move a dialog box to a different location on the screen move the mouse pointer to the box's *title bar* (the top line of the box), then hold down the pick button while moving the mouse pointer.

Dialog boxes include several tools for making decisions and selecting commands:

* *Multiple-choice boxes* present a limited number of available options, allowing you to select one, either by using the

mouse to pick the small button to the left of the option, or by holding down the Alt key and pressing the underlined letter in the option label. When an option is selected, the button to its left appears filled in.

- *Text boxes* appear either blank or filled in with a default response. These boxes allow you to enter a response from the keyboard. To make an entry in a text box, pick it with the mouse pointer (or hold down the Alt key and press the underlined letter in the text box label), then type your entry. Figure 2.2 illustrates text boxes for entering labels, column widths, and decimal places.

- *Toggle switches* include a label and a small rectangle to the left. Toggle switches allow you to activate or deactivate a

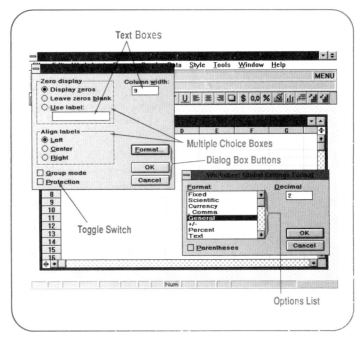

Figure 2.2: Dialog boxes

worksheet setting by picking the button with the mouse or by holding down the Alt key and pressing the underlined letter in the switch label. When a toggle switch is activated, an *X* fills the rectangle. When deactivated, the rectangle is empty. Figure 2.2 includes toggle switches for Group Mode (synchronizing format changes between multiple worksheets in the same file); Protection (prevents changes to cells); and Parentheses (encloses values in parentheses).

- *Option lists* present a series of options in a window in the dialog box. If the list is too long to fit in the window, a scroll bar appears to the right of the list. You may select an option by picking it with the mouse.

  If you are using the keyboard, you can activate the option list either by holding down the Alt key and pressing the underlined letter in the window's label or by pressing the Tab key until the list becomes active. Then, highlight the desired option using the arrow keys, and press Enter. Figure 2.2 includes an options list that allows you to select from among various cell formats.

- *Buttons* execute commands or open other dialog boxes. All dialog boxes include at least two buttons: one labeled *OK*, which activates the changes you have made and restores the original display; and *Cancel*, which restores the display without making any changes. You can "press" these buttons on the screen by picking them with the mouse. If you are using the keyboard, you can highlight the buttons in turn by pressing the Tab key. To pick the highlighted button, press Enter. In Figure 2.2, the dark line that surrounds the OK button in the lower-right dialog box indicates that the OK button is currently highlighted and will be picked if you press Enter.

This book makes frequent references to the *pick button*. The pick button is a mouse button and is used to select on-screen objects. It is not a screen button.

The Mode Indicator

The mode indicator tells you what 1-2-3 expects

The *mode indicator* is a highlighted box that appears near the upper-right corner of the screen, just below the menu bar. Lotus 1-2-3 shifts between many different modes (for example, EDIT, HELP, or READY) as it processes data, and a glance at the mode indicator will help you understand what to expect and what keystrokes or commands are appropriate at any given time. For information on 1-2-3's various processing modes, consult the 1-2-3 documentation.

Scroll Bars

Scroll bars help you move around in the worksheet

Use a *Scroll Bar* to move around the worksheet. The vertical scroll bar moves up or down (between rows) and the horizontal scroll bar moves right or left (between columns).

Each scroll bar contains a *scroll box* that moves within a narrow column at the border of the worksheet's window. To move the box, move the mouse pointer to it and hold the pick button down while moving the mouse. Release the pick button when the desired portion of the worksheet is displayed. You can also move around by clicking anywhere in the scroll bar—in the vertical scroll bar, this is the same as pressing the PgDn key; in the horizontal scroll bar, this is the same as the Tab key.

Alternatively, you can move the scroll box by clicking the arrow buttons at either end of the scroll bar. Holding the pick button down moves the scroll box along the scroll bar in the direction of the arrow. To stop the movement, release the pick button.

The Icon Palette

The icon palette contains frequently used 1-2-3 commands

The *icon palette* contains a series of buttons that correspond to 1-2-3 commands. If you are using a mouse, you may find it easier to simply pick one of these buttons rather than making repeated picks through the hierarchical menu structure.

For example, to load a worksheet, click the icon that shows a disk with an arrow pointing away from it. To save the current worksheet under its current name, press the icon button that shows a disk with an arrow pointing to it. This book will alert you to 1-2-3's icon-palette buttons when discussing the commands that they represent.

Status Indicators

The *status indicators* provide helpful information about the current state of the system: for example, when the Num Lock or Caps Lock keys are toggled on, or the current date and time. For more information about the status indicators and what they mean, consult your documentation.

Controlling the Windows

1-2-3 allows you to open many worksheet files at the same time—up to the limits of memory and storage space in your system. Each worksheet file is contained in its own window. If you are using a mouse, you can use standard Windows commands to manipulate these windows. A *window control menu box* is in the upper-left corner of each window. To display the window control menu, pick the control box with the mouse. This menu contains standard Windows commands for changing the size and location of individual windows.

1-2-3 uses standard Windows commands

Two standard Windows buttons appear in the upper-right corner of each worksheet window:

The *maximize* button is an upward-pointing arrow icon. If you pick this button with the mouse, the current window will fill the screen. To restore it to its previous size, open the Window Control menu and pick Restore.

The *minimize* button is a downward-pointing arrow icon. If you pick this button, the window will shrink down to an icon. This is useful for files that you want to keep in memory, but don't need to display all the time. To restore the window to its previous size, double-click on the icon.

You can change the size and location of the worksheet window using standard Windows techniques; for example, you can move a window by clicking the mouse pointer on any of its edges and then holding down the pick button while you move the mouse.

Moving around the Worksheet

To move around the worksheet, use 1-2-3's movement keys or the mouse pointer when 1-2-3 is in READY mode. If you only need to move one cell at a time, this is a simple operation: each time you press an arrow key, you move the cell pointer one cell in the direction indicated by the key. If you want to move further, you can move the mouse pointer to the desired cell and pick it, or you can use 1-2-3's speed keys. The following list describes some of 1-2-3's most commonly used speed keys:

- The Home key moves to cell A1 on the current layer.

- The Tab key moves you one screen to the right.

- Shift-Tab moves you one screen to the left.

- PgDn moves you one screen down.

- PgUp moves you one screen up.

On-Screen Help

You can access help for any 1-2-3 command by pressing F1. If you press F1 while in READY mode, an index of general help topics appears. Pick the desired topic using the mouse, or if you are using the keyboard, press the Tab key until the desired topic is highlighted, then press Enter. When you select a topic, 1-2-3 displays information on that topic.

Some information screens refer you to other related topics. These related topics appear highlighted within the help text, and can be selected as described in the previous paragraph. As you select topics, additional screens of information will appear. To display an earlier Help screen, pick the Back button with the mouse or press Alt-B. To return to 1-2-3, pick File from the menu bar, followed by Exit, or if using the keyboard, press Alt-FX.

The 1-2-3 Help feature is context sensitive; if you press F1 while in the middle of a command, 1-2-3 will display information about that command.

Quitting 1-2-3

To exit 1-2-3, pick File from the menu bar while in READY mode, followed by Exit. If you are using the keyboard, press Alt-FX. When you invoke the command to quit, 1-2-3 displays a small window asking if you would like to save all the currently open worksheet files before quitting. You can pick one of three buttons in response:

- *Yes*: Select this button to save worksheet data and quit.

- *No*: Select this button to quit without saving data.

- *Cancel*: Select this button to remain in 1-2-3; data in memory is not saved to disk.

Step 3

Entering Data

This step shows you how to enter data into the worksheet's cells. To gain practical experience in entering data, you will create a simple statement of income and expenses.

Labels, Values, and Formulas

There are three basic data types in 1-2-3:

- A *label* can be any set of alphanumeric characters not subject to mathematical analysis. Examples of labels are titles, headings, legends, explanatory text, and text fields in 1-2-3 databases.

- *Values* are any numeric data that can be subjected to mathematical calculations.

- *Formulas* instruct 1-2-3 to perform calculations on values in various areas of the spreadsheet and display the result. A *function* is a special type of formula that performs complex mathematical processes (such as internal rates of return) with a single, abbreviated command.

Data types

Entering Data

To enter data in a cell, move the cell pointer to that cell and type in your entry. The mode indicator then displays LABEL or VALUE, depending on the data you enter. For example, 1-2-3 displays VALUE if you begin by typing one of the following characters:

```
1 2 3 4 5 6 7 8 9 0 + - . ( @ # $
```

The numeric characters shown above represent numbers; the punctuation marks are special *reserved characters* that 1-2-3 uses to identify formulas and functions.

If you begin by typing a character other than a number or reserved character, 1-2-3 assumes that you are entering a label and the mode indicator changes accordingly.

Entering Labels

In most cases, creating a label is as easy as typing the text you want. For example, move the cell pointer to cell A1 and type the following:

```
Income/Expense Statement
```

As you type, the words appear in the *data area*, a line below the menu bar and to the right of the active cell address. As soon as 1-2-3 senses that you have entered data, two buttons appear to the left of the data line. If you pick the button with the *X* icon, you will cancel any input into the current cell. If you pick the button with the check icon, data is immediately copied from the data line to the active cell. You may also transfer data from the data line to the current cell by pressing Enter or by using one of the keyboard arrow keys to move the cell pointer.

For example, if you pick the check button, press Enter, or press an arrow key now, 1-2-3 places the words *Income/Expense Statement* in cell A1.

Because you did not begin this entry with a number or reserved character, 1-2-3 assumes it is a label and adds a *label prefix* automatically. The default prefix is an apostrophe ('), which indicates that the label is to be left-justified in the cell. Although you can see the label prefix in the data line, it is not visible in the worksheet.

From time to time, you may need to enter a label that begins with a number or reserved character. To do so, you must first type the label prefix yourself so that 1-2-3 will not mistake your entry for a value.

Unlike values, labels can overlap their cells

Although the label you just entered is wider than the cell, 1-2-3, in its default configuration, allows it to overlap adjacent blank cells. However, the entire label is considered to reside only in its original entry cell, and you must move the cell pointer to this cell if you wish to edit or delete it.

Try entering additional labels in cells so that your worksheet looks like Figure 3.1. Do not be concerned with the worksheet's appearance at this point. You will learn many ways to make the worksheet more attractive and readable in subsequent steps.

Inserting Numbers

Now let's complete the sample worksheet by entering some values. A value is entered with the same basic technique, but must begin with a number or reserved character.

Move the cell pointer to C4 and type **100000.** Do not enter commas, dollar signs, or any other formatting characters—this would cause 1-2-3 to display an error message. Press the ↓ key, and 1-2-3 will enter the number in the active cell and move the cell pointer. Add the remaining numbers so that the worksheet looks like Figure 3.2.

Certain characters, when entered with numbers, affect the way the numbers are stored in cells.

+   Stores the number as positive. This is the default; the sign is dropped when you enter the number. For example, *+100000* is stored as *100000.*

−   Stores the number as negative.

.   Stores the number with a decimal point. You can include only one decimal point in any given number.

%   Stores the number divided by 100; the sign is dropped. This character should follow the number. For example, *100000%* is stored as *1000.*

E   Stores the number in scientific notation. For example, *1E5* is stored as *100000.*

Numbers, unlike labels, are never allowed to overlap adjacent cells. If a number cannot fit in its cell and you have not indicated any special formatting for the cell, 1-2-3 will attempt to display the number in scientific notation. If you have formatted the cell or the

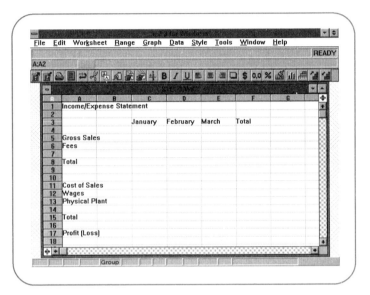

Figure 3.1: Sample worksheet with labels added

number is too long even for scientific notation, 1-2-3 fills the cell with asterisks (****). To make such numbers visible, you must change the format of the worksheet as described in upcoming steps.

Saving and Retrieving Files

The worksheet that appears on your monitor exists only in the computer's RAM. It is not automatically saved to disk. If you were to exit 1-2-3 or turn off the computer right now, you would lose your data. Therefore, it is important that you save your work often, and 1-2-3 for Windows gives you several means to do so.

To save the worksheet's data to disk, pick File from the menu bar, followed by Save or Save As.

If you have not yet saved the current worksheet to disk, 1-2-3 labels its window *Untitled.* When you pick File Save to save an untitled worksheet file, 1-2-3 supplies a default file name for the file: FILE*nnnn*.WK3, where *nnnn* is a number from 0001 to 9999.

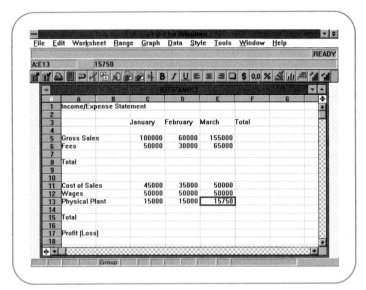

Figure 3.2: Sample worksheet with numbers added

If you want to give the file a more recognizable name, pick **File**, followed by Save As. If using the keyboard, press Alt-FA. A dialog box appears, offering a default name for the file in a text box. To erase the file name in the text box, simply begin typing the new file name, or press the Backspace key. When typing in a new file name, be sure to include the drive letter and subdirectory path if you want to store the file somewhere other than on the current default drive and subdirectory.

As with any 1-2-3 text box, you can edit its contents by using the ← key to move the editing cursor. Insert new characters by typing them in. Delete characters at the cursor position by pressing the Delete key, or backspace over characters by pressing the Backspace key.

Once a file is named, use the File Save command, or if using the keyboard, press Alt-FS. To save the data and at the same time close the worksheet file window, pick File from the menu bar, followed by Close. If using the keyboard, press Alt-FC. 1-2-3 will prompt you to save the file's data, offering three response buttons:

- *Yes:* Overwrites the file on disk with the current file and closes the file window.

- *No:* Discards the data and closes the worksheet file window.

- *Cancel:* Cancels the command, and returns to the worksheet on the screen.

Pick one of the buttons, or, if using the keyboard, press Tab to highlight each button in turn, pressing Enter to pick the highlighted button.

Unless you have no intention of saving your work, pick **File Save** often during your work session, thus keeping the file on disk up to date. This will prevent loss of data in the event of power failures or hardware glitches.

If you are using a mouse, you can use the icon palette to make file-saving easy: pick the icon button showing an arrow pointing towards the center of a disk.

Retrieving *files*

To retrieve a file, pick **File** from the menu bar, followed by **Open,** to open a new worksheet window. If you are using a mouse, you can pick the icon-palette button that shows an arrow pointing away from the center of a disk. Lotus 1-2-3 displays a dialog box that contains a text box in which you can type the name of the file you want to retrieve. This dialog box also contains a small window which displays the names of the worksheet files found on the current drive and subdirectory path. You can access this list directly using the mouse pointer, or, if you are using the keyboard, activate the list by pressing Alt-F.

Scroll through the list and highlight the desired file name using either the mouse pointer or the keyboard arrow keys. When the desired file is highlighted, double-click the pick button or press Enter.

The dialog box also contains two other small windows showing directories below the current default and a list of other available drive letters on your system. Unless the current directory is the root directory, the directory window will contain at least one other directory, the *parent directory,* which is the directory just above the current directory. The parent directory is represented by two dots (..) in the directory list. To change to any directory in this list, highlight and select it as described above for file names. If you are using the keyboard, activate the directory list by pressing Alt-D.

A list of available drives appears when you pick the button just to the right of the current default drive letter, or, if using the keyboard, press Alt-V and cycle through the available drives using the up- and down-arrow keys. You can change to a different drive using the highlight and selection techniques described earlier. When you have indicated the file you want, pick the OK button or press Enter. The file is loaded into memory, and displayed in a window on screen.

A 1-2-3 worksheet is flexible, providing you with a number of ways to present your data. *Formatting* the worksheet makes it attractive and readable.

The appearance of labels and values, both on the screen and in printed output, is determined by *format codes*, which can apply to individual cells, ranges of cells, or the entire worksheet. This step explains how 1-2-3's formatting codes change the look of your data and describes the commands that introduce these codes into your worksheet.

Value Formats

Value formats change the appearance of numbers. A value format will have no effect on a label. Figure 4.1 lists value format codes and their effect on various values.

Regardless of their format, values are displayed right-aligned in their cell. A blank space is always included after the value, as a buffer between the cell's data and any data in the cell to the right. A cell containing a value must be at least two characters wide.

Value Format Commands

Value formats are assigned to cells using 1-2-3 menu commands. You have two ways to change the value formats of cells: *globally,* in which the new format applies to all the cells in the worksheet, or *locally,* in which the new format applies only to specific ranges of cells or individual cells. Local formats take precedence over global ones; thus, different cells in the same worksheet can have different formats. However, any individual cell will have only one format code at a time.

Local formats override global formats

Changing Value Formats of Cells

To change the format of specific cells in a worksheet, first move the cell pointer to one corner of the range of cells you would like to format. Hold down the mouse button and move the cell pointer to the opposite corner of the range of cells. If you are using the keyboard, press the F4 function key, then move the cell pointer to the opposite corner of the range using the keyboard's arrow keys. If you are formatting only a single cell, simply move the cell pointer to that cell.

Pick **R**ange from the menu bar, followed by **F**ormat. A dialog box prompts you for one of the format types listed in Figure 4.1. If you select a format that includes decimal places, use the text box to indicate the number of decimal places. You may also activate the Parentheses toggle switch if you would like values to be displayed

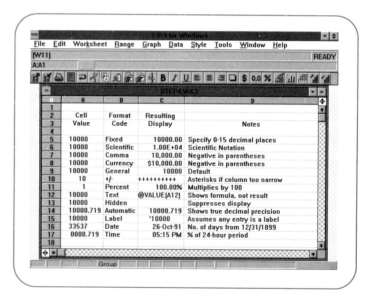

Figure 4.1: Value formats

within parentheses. By default, negative values are always displayed within parentheses when using the Currency and Comma formats.

When you pick the OK button, the indicated range is formatted.

Global Value Formatting

Let's try formatting the Income/Expense worksheet that you created in the previous step. To format the worksheet globally, pick Worksheet from the menu bar, followed by Global Settings. The Global Settings dialog box appears, which was illustrated in Figure 2.2. To change the global format setting, pick the button labeled Format, or press Alt-F. This displays another dialog box similar to the dialog box displayed when you picked the Range Format command. As described earlier, pick the Fixed format and enter **2** in the text-entry window for the number of decimal places, then pick the OK button or press Enter. The worksheet labels will remain unchanged, but all the values will now be displayed with two decimal places.

Some columns may be too narrow for the newly formatted values to fit in their cells, in which case asterisks will appear. You will solve that formatting problem just ahead.

Changing Column Widths

You can further modify the appearance of your worksheet by changing the width of the columns. The default column width is nine characters. Although labels are not usually affected by column width, values often are. A column must always be at least one character wider than the largest value it holds, because the last character is always blank.

1-2-3's default value format is General.

As with other types of formatting, you can change column widths either globally (the whole worksheet) or locally (one column at a time).

You can globally change column widths by picking Worksheet from the menu bar, followed by Global Settings. When the dialog box appears, pick the text-entry window labeled *Column width* and enter the new column width. Then pick the OK button or press Enter. All columns in the worksheet are assigned the new width except for those that have already been assigned a width locally.

To use the menus to change the width of specific columns, first highlight the range of columns you want to change, using the range-highlighting techniques described earlier. The number of highlighted rows in this case is irrelevant, since only the highlighted columns will be affected.

Pick Worksheet from the menu bar, followed by Column width. When the dialog box appears, pick the multiple-choice button labeled Set width to, if it is not already highlighted, then enter the desired width in the text box. The column width is expressed as the maximum number of characters that can fit in that column's cell.

After you have entered the number of characters for the column width, pick the OK button or press Enter, and 1-2-3 changes the column width.

You can use the mouse to "show" 1-2-3 how wide to make any single column. To do this, move the pointer to the right border line of the column heading, located in the column border area of the worksheet. When you do this, the pointer icon changes to a double arrow. Now press the pick button and hold it down as you move the mouse horizontally. A dotted vertical line appears on the worksheet, moving as you move the pointer. This line indicates the new width of the column. When the line is in the correct position, release the pick button, and the column width is changed.

Let's try changing the width of the columns in the Income/Expense worksheet. Pick Worksheet Global Settings and enter a new column width of **10**. This will allow you to format the columns with two decimal places and keep all the values visible in the worksheet. The newly formatted statement is illustrated in Figure 4.2.

Label Formats

As you can see from Figure 4.2, changing the column widths caused the month headings to appear misaligned. To line up the month headings in their columns, you must change the *label format* in these cells.

When you format a label, you are changing its position within the cell. Format codes for labels take the form of special *label prefixes* that must be placed before the affected entries. Figure 4.3 shows how each of the 1-2-3 label prefixes affects the display.

Use label prefixes to change label formats

Label Format Commands

Each label in the worksheet has a label prefix. Unless you indicate otherwise, 1-2-3 assumes that labels are left-justified. If this is how you want a label to appear, then you can enter it without a prefix;

		1-2-3 for Windows			▼ ◆
File	Edit	Worksheet	Range	Graph	Data	Style	Tools	Window	Help

READY

A:A2

	A	B	C	D	E	F	G	
1	Income/Expense Statement							
2								
3		January	February	March	Total			
4								
5	Gross Sales		100000.00	60000.00	155000.00			
6	Fees		50000.00	30000.00	65000.00			
7								
8	Total							
9								
10								
11	Cost of Sales		45000.00	35000.00	50000.00			
12	Wages		50000.00	50000.00	50000.00			
13	Physical Plant		15000.00	15000.00	15750.00			
14								
15	Total							
16								
17	Profit (Loss)							
18								

STEP4.WK3

Group

Figure 4.2: The Income/Expense Statement, with fixed-decimal format

1-2-3 will add the apostrophe prefix for you. Otherwise, type the label prefix as the first character in the label.

To change the default label prefix, pick Worksheet from the menu bar, followed by Global Settings. When the Global Settings dialog box appears, pick the desired default from the multiple-choice list titled *Align Labels*. You can choose either left, center, or right alignment. When you have made your selection, pick the OK button or press Enter. When you change the label-prefix default, labels that have already been added to the worksheet are not changed.

You can also change the formats of labels that you have already entered. Begin by highlighting the range of cells you would like to reformat, then pick Style from the menu bar, followed by Alignment. Pick the desired label alignment (left, centered, or right) from the

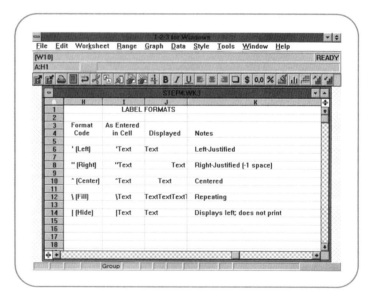

Figure 4.3: Label formats

multiple-choice list in the dialog box. Pick the OK button or press Enter to complete the reformatting process. Cells containing values are not formatted.

Let's format the labels in row 3 of the Income/Expense worksheet. Move the cell pointer to cell C3, labeled *January.* Hold down the mouse's pick button (or press F4 if using the keyboard), then move the cell pointer to cell F3, highlighting the range. If you are using the keyboard, press Enter after highlighting the range to return 1-2-3 to READY mode.

Next, pick Style Alignment, then pick Center from the *Align Label* list. Then pick the OK button or press Enter again. 1-2-3 then realigns the labels in row 3. If you like, you can indent the *Total* labels in column A by moving the cell pointer to those labels and repeating the sequence, selecting Right from the *Align Label* list.

The label prefix for a repeating label cannot be assigned with menu commands. To create labels with these prefixes, type the prefix just before typing the label.

The repeating label prefix is often used to draw lines. For example, to draw a line across a cell in the current worksheet, move the cell pointer to C7 and type the repeating label prefix (\) and a hyphen. Press Enter, and the cell will fill with hyphens, creating a line.

If you would like to extend this line, you can enter the same label in cells D7 and E7. You can draw another line in cells C14, D14, and E14. (In Step 9, you will learn how to copy cells, which is a more efficient way of extending lines across many columns.)

The sample worksheet should now look like Figure 4.4.

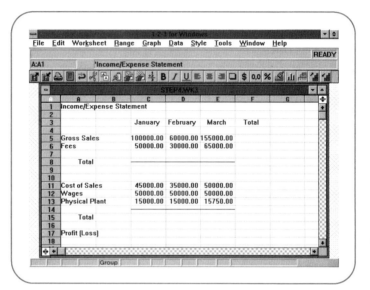

Figure 4.4: The Income/Expense Statement, with label formats added

Creating Formulas

A *formula* is an instruction to 1-2-3 to process specified data. Formulas in 1-2-3 consist of three fundamental elements: operators, numbers, and cell addresses.

An *operator* is a symbol for the type of processing that you want to do. The plus sign (+) is an example of an operator; it indicates either that a number is positive or that 1-2-3 is to add numbers together. If you move the cell pointer to an empty cell in the worksheet and type

5+9

1-2-3 displays the result of the addition, *14,* in the cell.

The real power of 1-2-3 becomes evident when you add cell addresses to formulas. This allows you to reference values in other cells. When you combine cell addresses and operators, 1-2-3 takes the data it finds in the referenced cells and performs the requested processing, displaying the result of the processing in the formula's cell. Thereafter, any change to the contents of the referenced cells will cause the result of the formula to change as well. This is the basic technique for using the worksheet to perform what-if analyses.

Referencing cells

Entering Formulas in the Worksheet

Let's use the Income/Expense Statement that you formatted in Step 4 to gain some practical experience with formulas. Move the cell pointer to cell C8 and enter the following, exactly as shown:

+C5+C6

The program adds the values in cells C5 and C6 and displays the result, *150000,* in cell C8. If you find that 1-2-3 does not update the result immediately, press F9 to recalculate the worksheet. The reason for doing this will be discussed later on in this step under the heading *Manual Recalculation.*

Notice that the formula you entered begins with a plus sign (+) operator. This operator is extremely important for two reasons:

- It tells 1-2-3 that you are entering a formula, not a label. 1-2-3 would have assumed it was a label if you had simply begun with the letter C.

- It tells 1-2-3 that the number referenced in cell C5 is to be treated as positive.

A formula can begin with other operators as required. For example, given the original values in cells C5 and C6, if you had entered

`-C5+C6`

1-2-3 would have displayed $-50,000.00$, the result of adding -100000 and 50000. A complete list of formula operators can be found in Table 5.1.

Order of Precedence	Operator	Function	Example (A2= 9 A3=5)	Result
1	^	Exponentiation	+A2^3	729
2	+	Positive Value	+A2	9
2	−	Negative Value	−A2	−9
3	*	Multiplication	+A2*A3	45
3	/	Division	+A2/A3	1.8
4	+	Addition	+A2+A3	14
4	−	Subtraction	+A2−A3	4

Table 5.1: Numeric Operators

Formulas use numbers literally

In addition to cell references and operators, a formula can contain numbers. For example, the following is a valid formula:

`30000+C5`

The program will display the result of adding *30000* to the value referenced in cell C5. An operator is not needed at the beginning of this example because the formula begins with a number, so 1-2-3 knows you are not trying to enter a label.

A formula is limited to 512 characters, but within this limit you can combine operators, cell addresses, and numbers. This gives you the ability to create quite complex formulas.

Precedence

Operator *precedence* refers to the order in which numeric operators are evaluated in a formula. Table 5.1 lists the numeric operators in their order of precedence. Thus, in formulas that contain more than one numeric operator, exponentiation is evaluated first, followed by positive or negative values, followed by multiplication and division, followed by addition and subtraction.

The order of operator precedence is extremely important to keep in mind when you are entering formulas that contain more than one kind of numeric operator; if you don't, you may not get the results you intended.

If you cannot achieve the desired results with 1-2-3's internal order of operator precedence, you can use parentheses to spell out to 1-2-3 exactly in what order to perform the calculations in formulas. For example, if you type the equation

Using parentheses

```
(5+9)*3
```

1-2-3 will suspend the normal order of precedence and perform the addition first, then the multiplication.

Using the Cell Pointer to Create Formulas

So far, you have entered cell addresses in formulas by typing them in at the keyboard. Alternatively, you can "show" 1-2-3 the cells you intend to include in formulas by moving the cell pointer to them.

For example, to enter a formula that will add cells C5 and C6 in the Income/Expense Statement, move the cell pointer to cell C8 and enter a plus sign, just as if you were entering another formula. However, instead of typing in the cell address, move the cell pointer to C5. You can use the arrow keys to move the cell pointer, or if you like, you can pick cell C5 using the mouse pointer.

Notice that the active cell address is automatically referenced in the data line as you move the pointer. When you use the arrow keys, 1-2-3 references the cell address in the data line, as follows:

+A:C5

However, when you pick the cell using the mouse pointer, 1-2-3 references the cell in the data line as a *range* that encompasses only one cell, as follows:

+A:C5..A:C5

Both of these references are functionally the same with regard to the formula's result.

When you have moved the cell pointer to C5, type another plus sign. The cell pointer now returns to the original cell (C8) and awaits your next entry. Again, move the cell pointer, this time to cell C6. Notice how 1-2-3 again references the active cell address in the data line as you move the pointer.

When you have moved the pointer to cell C6, the formula in the data line is complete. The data line should read:

+A:C5+A:C6

Or, if you picked cells using the mouse pointer, it will read:

+A:C5..A:C5+A:C6..A:C6

This is the formula you want, so press Enter. 1-2-3 places the formula in cell C8 and calculates the result.

You can create long formulas without typing cell addresses using this method. Remember that you must add an operator before each cell address. Do not press Enter until the formula is complete.

For practice, try entering formulas for the remaining five columns in the Income/Expense worksheet. You can also use formulas to fill out the Profit/(Loss) line in the worksheet. The formula for this line in the *January* column is cell C8 minus cell C15:

```
+A:C8-A:C15
```

Enter similar formulas for columns D and E. Try using both the cell pointer and the keypad to input the correct cell addresses. When you are finished entering all the formulas, the worksheet should look like Figure 5.1.

Nesting Formulas

It is possible to write formulas that include cell addresses of cells that contain other formulas. If you write such formulas, the result of the referenced formula is used in the current formula.

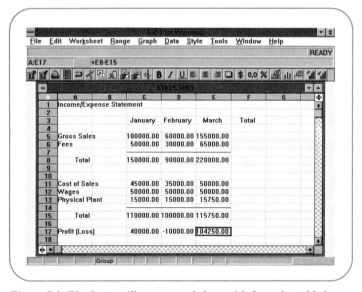

Figure 5.1: The Income/Expense worksheet with formulas added

You have already done this with the formula in the Profit/Loss line. Note that the formula in cell C17 references cell C8 and C15. Both these cells contain formulas. C17 then displays the result of subtracting the result of the formula in C15 from the result of the formula in C8.

Errors in Formulas

If you enter an invalid formula (for example, two operators without a number or cell address between them), 1-2-3 will switch to EDIT mode to allow you to make changes to the formula. You will learn more about editing data in Step 7. However, if the formula is simple, like the examples in this step, you can press the Delete key to erase the formula in the active cell and start over.

If you make changes to your worksheet that make a formula invalid (for example, if you erase a referenced cell or replace its contents with data the formula cannot interpret), 1-2-3 will display the symbol ERR, right-aligned in the formula's cell. This alerts you that the formula is now invalid. When you see this symbol, you must change or replace the formula in that cell.

Circular References

As your formulas become increasingly complex, it is possible to create a formula that references itself. Such a self-referencing formula is called a *circular reference,* meaning that it can never be resolved.

When a circular reference occurs in the worksheet, 1-2-3 displays the *Circ* symbol in the status indicator line to alert you. Certain financial analyses require circular references (for example, deducting a percentage of a net profit, which in turn reduces the net profit), but in many cases, a circular reference is an error.

When formulas become complex, circular references can be hard to find. To get assistance in eliminating a circular reference, pick **Help** from the menu bar, followed by About 1-2-3. If you are using the keyboard, press Alt-HA. The resulting display will include the cell address of one of the formulas in the circular reference. Analyze the formula in this cell and the cells to which it refers to track down the circular reference.

Manual Recalculation

By default, 1-2-3 will update formulas whenever data in a referenced cell is changed. If you are adding or changing many cells in a large worksheet with lots of formulas, you might find the constant process of updating annoying or inconvenient. You can turn off the automatic recalculation feature by picking Tools from the menu bar, followed by User Setup. If you are using the keyboard, press Alt-TU. 1-2-3 displays a dialog box of setup options, which include a button labeled *Recalculation.* If you pick this button or press Alt-R, 1-2-3 displays a second dialog box, which includes a multiple-choice box that allows you to choose between Automatic or Manual recalculation. Pick the circular button to the left of the Manual option or press Alt-M, then pick the OK button or press Enter.

F9 recalculates the worksheet

To make this change permanent, pick the Update button or press Alt-U. To return to the worksheet, pick the OK button. If you are using the keyboard, press the Tab key until the OK button is highlighted, then press Enter.

Thereafter, any change you make to the worksheet will cause the *Calc* symbol to appear in the status indicator line, alerting you that the worksheet may need to be recalculated. After making your changes, press the F9 function key, and all the formulas will be updated. The *Calc* symbol will disappear until your next change to the worksheet.

Step 6

Using Functions

A *function* is a special type of formula that performs complex operations that would be difficult or impossible to do using a simple formula alone. For example, if you wanted to add up a series of 100 cells, you could do so with a long formula referencing each cell address. However, this would be a tedious process at best and prone to error as well.

Lotus 1-2-3 uses *functions* in situations like this. For example, the function that adds a long series of values is @SUM. This step shows you how to use such functions.

Function Syntax

All 1-2-3 functions begin with the *function symbol,* also known as the "at" symbol (@). This symbol alerts 1-2-3 that you are using a function. The *function name* follows the function symbol and identifies what it does. Function names are not case-sensitive; you can use either uppercase or lowercase.

The function name is followed by a list of *function parameters,* which can include cell addresses, ranges of cell addresses, strings, numbers, formulas, or even other functions, depending on what is required.

Function parameters

The function parameters are enclosed in parentheses. Some parameters, such as formulas or other functions, can be nested within their own pairs of parentheses. When more than one pair of parentheses occurs within the list of function parameters, the data within the innermost pair is evaluated first, the data within the next innermost pair is evaluated second, and so on, until the outermost pair of parentheses is reached.

For example, the following function, which totals a range of 100 cells starting with cell A1 and ending with cell B50, illustrates the basic syntax for all functions:

`@SUM(A:A1..A:B50)`

It begins with the at symbol (@), which is followed by the function name, in this case, *SUM*. The function's parameters are enclosed in a single set of parentheses immediately after the function name.

Ranges in functions

The @SUM function requires the address of at least a single cell but frequently uses a range of cells. Whenever a function operates on a range of cells, the starting and ending cell addresses are separated by two periods.

In the above example, the starting cell is A1 and the ending cell is B50. The function, therefore, adds the values in all cells in rows 1 through 50 that are in columns A and B.

Placing Functions in Cells

You enter functions in cells using the same techniques you use to enter simple formulas. You begin by typing the @ symbol. Then type the function name and the opening parenthesis.

Thereafter, if a cell address is required, you can type it in or move the cell pointer to the required cell. Finally, type in any other required parameters.

If you are entering a range of cells using the keyboard, enter the starting cell address and follow it with a period. You need enter only one period; 1-2-3 will make it two periods when you finish creating the formula. After entering the period, type the ending cell address or move the cell pointer to the range's ending cell.

If you are using the mouse pointer, you can indicate the range by picking the starting cell, holding the pick button down, and moving the cell pointer to the ending cell. The program will scroll the worksheet for you if you move the cell pointer to the edge of the worksheet's window.

When you have finished entering the function's parameters, enter the closing parenthesis, and the function is complete. Press Enter to place the function in the cell or pick the check button to the left of the data line.

The following example uses the Income/Expense worksheet that you have used in previous steps. Place the cell pointer in cell F5 and type the following, but do not press Enter afterward:

`@SUM(`

Now, to enter the range of cells to sum, move the cell pointer to cell C5. Notice how 1-2-3 updates the formula in the control panel as you move the cell pointer.

When you reach cell C5, type a period if using the keyboard or hold down the pick button if using the mouse. This indicates to 1-2-3 that the current cell is the starting cell of the range to be summed. Now move the cell pointer two cells to the right to E5. Notice that 1-2-3 highlights the current range of cells as you move the pointer. Also, 1-2-3 updates the cell range in the control panel, showing the starting and ending cells of the highlighted range.

When you have highlighted the range C5..E5, type the closing parenthesis to complete the function. The cell pointer then moves to the original entry cell, F5. Press Enter to place the function in that cell. 1-2-3 then sums C5 through E5 and displays the result. Your worksheet should look like the one illustrated in Figure 6.1.

If you like, you can practice entering functions by moving the cell pointer down the cells in column F and repeating the above process for the other rows in the worksheet. However, you will return to this worksheet in Step 8 and learn a better way to append formulas to a range of cells by replicating a single cell's function across a range.

Multiple Parameters

If a function contains more than one parameter (for example, a number plus a range of cells), separate the parameters with a comma.

Using commas in functions

Do not type a space after the comma—spaces are not allowed in functions. It is up to you to enter the correct number of parameters as required by the function you are using.

For example, consider @ROUND, another frequently used function. This function, as its name implies, rounds off numbers to a specific set of decimal places. It requires two parameters: the number to be rounded (or a cell address containing the number) and the number of decimal places of precision. The following example of this function rounds the value found in cell A3 to two decimal places:

> `@ROUND(A3,2)`

Notice that the cell address is followed by a comma, which is then followed by a number. The number *2* in this example indicates that the value in A3 is rounded to two decimal places. The result is displayed in the cell containing this function.

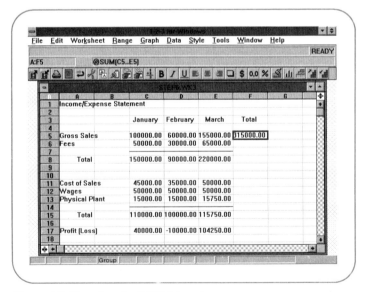

Figure 6.1: Entering the @SUM function

You could use this function to round off the result of other calculations. For example, consider the following nested function:

`@ROUND(@SUM(A1..B50),2)`

This function sums the cells A1 through B50, rounds the result to two decimal places, and places the final result in the cell containing the function.

Mixing Parameter Types

So far, you have seen examples of functions that use cell addresses, ranges, and numbers. Many functions allow you to mix parameter types and still display a correct result. For example, in addition to the parameters shown previously, all of the following are valid parameters for the @SUM function:

```
@SUM(1,2,3,4)
@SUM(A1,A2,A3,A4)
@SUM(A1..A50,B51..B100)
@SUM(A1+B1,A2..B50,100)
```

When in doubt about the particular parameter mix acceptable to a function, consult the 1-2-3 documentation. This will save you considerable time. However, don't be afraid to experiment. Experimentation can be an effective learning tool.

Function Types

Lotus 1-2-3 includes dozens of predefined functions. Some of the more commonly used types of functions are described in the following list. However, a book of this length can only hint at 1-2-3's capabilities. For a more complete list of the 1-2-3 functions, consult your documentation.

- Math functions supplement formulas for performing mathematical analyses. For example, @SQRT computes a number's square root.

- Financial functions perform business-related financial analyses. For example, @PMT computes loan payments.

- Statistical functions perform mathematical analyses on a value or series of values. For example, @AVG computes the average of a series of values.

- Logical functions perform tests on data and return values based on the results of the tests. For example, @IF tests a given condition. If the condition evaluates to TRUE, 1-2-3 performs a do-if-true function. Otherwise, 1-2-3 performs a do-if-false function.

From time to time, you will want to change data you have entered in a cell. The simplest method is to move the cell pointer to the cell and re-enter the data from scratch—the preferred method when the cell contains relatively simple data. However, if the cell contains a complicated formula or a long label, it is more efficient to *edit* the data. This step explains the basic techniques for editing your worksheet.

Editing a Cell's Contents

To perform simple editing on a cell, move the cell pointer to the desired cell and press the F2 key. Notice that the mode indicator changes from READY to EDIT and a special text-editing cursor appears in the data line. Alternatively, if you are using a mouse, you can move the pointer into the data line and click once.

As you move the cell pointer around the worksheet, 1-2-3 continually updates the data line to display the contents of the active cell. Once in EDIT mode, you can use the ← or → key to position a special *edit cursor* anywhere in the cell's characters, or, if the cell contains lengthy information, you can move the mouse pointer to the desired location and click once. When you have positioned the cursor where you want it, simply type in the new characters.

EDIT mode

To delete a single character to the right of the editing cursor, press the Delete key once. Press the Backspace key to delete the character to the left of the cursor. To delete a string of characters, position the cursor to the left of the first character in the string and then move the cursor to the ending character while holding down the pick button. The string will be highlighted and you can press the delete key to erase the entire string at once.

To update the worksheet with the edited data, press Enter or pick the ✓–icon button to the left of the data line. To abort editing without making changes, pick the X–icon button to the left of the data line.

For example, suppose you would like to insert the words *1st Quarter* into the title of the Income/Expense worksheet.

1. Move the cell pointer to cell A1 and press the F2 key. This switches 1-2-3 into EDIT mode and displays the phrase *Income/Expense Statement* in the data line.

2. Move the edit cursor to just before the *I* in *Income*.

3. Type **1st Quarter** and a space, then press Enter. The string is added to the label, the new label is displayed in the cell, and 1-2-3 returns to READY mode.

Moving Data

You may also want to move your data from one cell to another. Using 1-2-3 menu commands, you can move the data in either single cells or entire ranges of cells.

Moving a cell

To move data from one cell to another, begin by moving the cell pointer to the cell with the data you want to move. Then pick **Edit** from the menu bar, followed by **M**ove Cells. The Edit Move Cells dialog box appears, indicating the current cell in a text box labeled *From* and a default target location in a text box labeled *To.* You can see an example of this dialog box in Figure 7.1.

In this example, notice that the *To* text box in the Edit Move Cells dialog box contains a range whose beginning and ending cells are the same; this is the standard way for 1-2-3 to identify a single cell. You can change both the source and target cells by picking the appropriate text box with the mouse pointer, and typing in the desired cell address. If you are using the keyboard, pick the *From* box by pressing Alt-F and the *To* box by pressing Alt-T. You can also move between the text boxes and the buttons by pressing the Tab key.

If you are using a mouse and the source or target cells are visible on the screen, you can "show" 1-2-3 the desired cells by moving the mouse pointer to them and pressing the pick button. In order for this

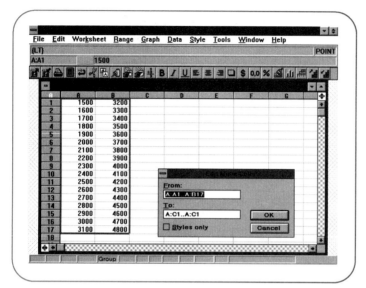

Figure 7.1: Moving the range A1..B17

technique to work, however, the edit cursor in the selected text box must be positioned just after the highlighted character string. If you are using the keyboard, you must type the correct target cell address in the *To* text box.

Press Enter or pick the OK button, and 1-2-3 relocates the data.

If you are using a mouse and the dialog box is covering the cell you want to pick, you can move it out of the way as follows: move the mouse pointer to the dialog box's title bar (Edit Move Cells). Hold the pick button down and move the mouse pointer. The dialog box will follow the pointer to a new location on the screen.

The above technique for moving data works well when the source and target cells are visible on the screen. If you want to move data between cells that are too far apart to appear on the screen together, though, you can do so by first moving the cell data to the Windows clipboard, then moving the cell pointer to the target cell, and finally pasting the data from the clipboard into the new location.

Cut-and-paste moving

The command sequence for accomplishing this is as follows:

1. Move the cell pointer to the cell whose data you intend to move.

2. Pick **Edit** from the menu bar, followed by **Cut.** If you are using the keyboard, hold down the Shift key and press the Delete key once, or press Alt-ET. The data disappears from the cell and is stored in the Windows clipboard.

3. Move the cell pointer to the target cell.

4. If you are using a mouse, pick **Edit** from the menu bar, followed by **Paste,** or pick the icon-palette button with the open bottle of paste. The previously cut data now appears in the target cell. If you are using the keyboard, you can accomplish the same thing by holding down the Shift key and pressing the Insert key once, or by pressing Alt-EP.

Moving a range

The technique for moving a range of cells is similar to that for moving a single cell. Start by moving the cell pointer to the upper-left corner of the range you would like to move. Once you have the cell pointer positioned correctly, hold down the mouse's pick button and move the cell pointer to the opposite corner of the range.

If you are using the keyboard, first press the F4 function key, then move the cell pointer with the arrow keys. As you move the cell pointer, the range will be highlighted. When you have finished highlighting the desired range, use the data-moving commands as described previously, indicating the highlighted range as the source cells.

To specify a destination for a range of cells, you need indicate only a single cell address, which 1-2-3 will use as the new upper-left corner of the range. The remaining cells in the range will be moved into positions relative to this cell.

For example, consider the list of numbers shown in the worksheet in Figure 7.1. To move the cells in the range A1 through B17 to the cells starting with C1, do the following:

1. Move the cell pointer to cell A1, then highlight cells A1 through B17 as described earlier in this section. The highlighted cells should look like those in Figure 7.1.

2. Pick Edit, followed by Move Cells. The dialog box should appear, as seen in Figure 7.1.

3. If necessary, move the dialog box as described previously. Now, pick the *To* text box, making sure the text cursor is positioned after the text string in the box and the string is highlighted.

4. Pick cell C1.

5. Press Enter (or pick the OK button) to eliminate the dialog box and move the cells. Your screen should now look like Figure 7.2.

Be careful when moving ranges of cells. If any part of the range overlaps cells that already contain data, the original data will be overwritten by the data that you have moved.

If you are moving long labels that overlap adjacent cells, it is not necessary to highlight all the visible text. To move labels, you need highlight only those cells where the labels were typed. In this regard, a quick glance at the data line as you move the cell pointer is useful, because it constantly displays the contents of the active cell while you move the pointer. Don't move empty cells if you can avoid it, since you might overwrite data at the destination.

Using Undo

It is possible that, in the course of editing data, you might make changes to your worksheet that you did not intend. The Undo feature allows you to reverse the effects of erroneous commands.

The simplest means of undoing a command sequence is to press Alt-Backspace or use the icon palette: pick the button with the semi-circle with the two arrowheads to undo the effects of the last command.

If you can do without the Undo feature, you can disable it, thereby increasing the amount of memory available for your spreadsheets. Pick **Tools** from the menu bar, followed by **User Setup**. The User Setup dialog box contains a toggle switch labeled *Enable Edit Undo*. If an *X* appears in the box to the left, Edit Undo is enabled. If this box is empty, Edit Undo is disabled. To toggle Edit Undo, pick the rectangular box to the left of the label.

Undo works only on the previous command. You cannot step back through a series of commands using Undo. If you need to undo more than one mistake, restore the worksheet from the backup copy.

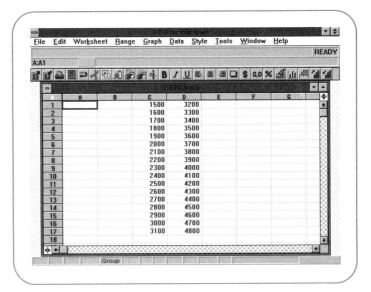

Figure 7.2: The result of moving range A1..B17 to C1

Step 8

Copying & Erasing Data

In addition to the editing techniques you have seen so far, editing worksheet data can involve copying it from one cell to another, making multiple copies, or simply erasing it. This step explains how to make these kinds of changes.

Copying Data

You can copy data from a single cell or a range of cells.

The basic technique for copying is almost the same as that for moving. To copy data from one cell to another, begin by moving the cell pointer to the cell containing the data you want to copy. Pick Edit from the menu bar, followed by Quick Copy. 1-2-3 displays the Edit Quick Copy dialog box, indicating the current cell in a text box labeled *From* and a default target location in a text box labeled *To*.

You can change both the source and target cells by picking the text box with the mouse pointer and typing in the desired cell address. If you are using the keyboard, pick the *From* box by pressing Alt-F and the *To* box by pressing Alt-T. You can also move between the text boxes, toggle switches, and buttons by pressing the Tab key.

If you are using a mouse and the source or target cells are visible on the screen, you can "show" 1-2-3 the desired cells by moving the mouse pointer to them and pressing the pick button (or Enter, if you are using the keyboard). In order for this technique to work, however, the edit cursor in the selected text box must be positioned just after the character string. If you are using the keyboard, you must type the correct target cell address in the *To* text box.

Press Enter or pick the OK button, and 1-2-3 copies the data in the new location.

Cut-and-paste copying

The previous technique for copying data works well when the source and target cells are visible on the screen. If you want to move data between cells that are located too far apart to appear on the screen together, you can do so by copying the cell data to the Windows clipboard, moving the cell pointer to the target cell, and pasting the data from the clipboard into the new location.

The command sequence for accomplishing this is as follows:

1. Move the cell pointer to the cell whose data you want to copy.

2. If you are using a mouse, pick Edit from the menu bar, followed by Copy. If you are using the keyboard, hold down the Ctrl key and press the Insert key once, or press Alt-EC. The data is now copied to the Windows clipboard.

3. Move the cell pointer to the target cell.

4. If using a mouse, pick Edit from the menu bar, followed by Paste. If you are using the keyboard, you can accomplish the same thing by holding down the Shift key and pressing the Insert key once, or by pressing Alt-EP.

Replicating Data

You can use the same technique to replicate data throughout a range of cells. To replicate cells, select a single cell to copy and the range where you want to replicate the selected cell. The program places a copy of the selected cell in each cell of the destination range.

The replication feature works on all types of data in cells, but it is most useful when copying formulas and functions. For example, you can use this technique to replicate the @SUM function that you entered in cell F5 of the Income/Expense Statement.

1. Move the cell pointer to F5, highlighting the cell.

2. Pick Edit followed by Quick Copy.

3. If you are using the menu, pick the data-entry box labeled *To,* highlighting its contents. Be sure the editing cursor is located just after the cell address in the box.

4. Move the mouse pointer down to cell F6, and hold down the pick button.

5. Move the mouse pointer to cell F17, highlighting the range.

6. Release the pick button, and the dialog box reappears, showing the indicated target range in the data-entry box. If you are using the icon palette, the data will be replicated immediately.

   If you are using the keyboard, simply type the correct target range into the *To* text box: **F6..F17**.

7. Press Enter (or pick the OK button), and 1-2-3 copies the formula in cell F5 throughout the target range. The totals in each row are displayed. Your worksheet should look like the worksheet in Figure 8.1.

Notice that the function has been replicated into rows where there are no values to sum. The functions in these cells return zero. Do not be concerned with this for the time being; you will eliminate these superfluous functions shortly.

Copying Formulas and Functions

When you move or copy formulas and functions in 1-2-3, you make use of one of its most remarkable features: *relative cell addressing.* This means that when you move or copy formulas or functions, 1-2-3 will automatically update their cell references to account for their new locations.

Relative cell addresses

To see how relative cell addressing works in the Income/Expense worksheet, move the cell pointer up through the functions you have just replicated and study each cells' contents as displayed in the top line of the control panel. You will notice that 1-2-3 has automatically updated the row numbers in each function to reflect its current location. This assures that the function will sum the values found in the function's current row, not the original row (which is what you might have reasonably expected, since you were making copies).

To understand relative cell addressing, you must understand how 1-2-3 looks at cell addresses in formulas. By default, 1-2-3 pays closer attention to the relative positions of a cell reference in a formula than it does to an *absolute* cell address; it displays the cell address more as a convenience to the user. Thus, when you move or copy a formula, you move or copy the reference to another relative location, not to an absolute cell address. The cell addresses in the display are changed because the formula, once relocated, is referencing different cells.

Most of the time, this feature is a great convenience, as it eliminates the need to enter each formula from scratch or update a formula each time it is copied. In some cases, though, you may want to copy a formula while retaining its reference to a particular cell.

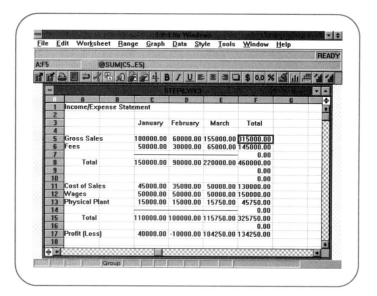

Figure 8.1: Replicating functions in the worksheet

1-2-3 allows you to change any relative cell address to an absolute address by including special codes in the cell address. Just add a dollar sign ($) in front of the layer letter, column letter, and row number, as in the following example:

    +$A:$B$3

The dollar signs signal 1-2-3 that it is not to change the cell address of B3 when the formula is relocated. Now, if you were to move the formula back one column to the left, it would still read

    +$A:$B$3

You have a lot of flexibility in defining what parts of the cell reference are absolute and relative. For example,

    +$A:$B3

will prevent the layer or column from changing, but allow the row to be updated. Likewise,

    +A:B$3

will prevent the row from changing, but allow the layer and column to be updated.

1-2-3 also provides a simple means of changing cell addresses in formulas from relative to absolute and back again. Start by moving the cell pointer to cell F9 in the Income/Expense Statement. The function in this cell should read

    @SUM(C9..E9)

Press the F2 key to enter EDIT mode, then press the F4 key. Notice the change in the display:

    @SUM($A:$C$9..$A:$E$9)

As you repeatedly press the F4 key, the cell addresses in the range will cycle through all possible combinations of relative and absolute addressing. When you have toggled to the addressing scheme that you want, press Enter.

*Absolute
cell
addresses*

*F4 cycles
through
address
formats*

The F4 function key works differently if you are editing a simple formula, such as the formula in cell C8:

+C5+C6

In this case, you need to move the cursor to a position within or just to the right of the characters in the cell address before pressing the F4 function key. When editing a simple formula, the function key will change only the cell address at the current cursor position.

Erasing Data

When you replicated the functions in column F of the Income/Expense worksheet, you placed copies in cells where they were not needed. You can choose from among several convenient erasing techniques to delete these superfluous functions, as demonstrated in the following sequence:

1. Move the cell pointer to F7.

2. Press the Delete key.

3. Move the cell pointer to F9.

4. Highlight the range F9..F10.

5. Press the Delete key.

6. Move the cell pointer to F14.

7. Press Shift-Delete (which moves the cell contents to the clipboard).

8. Move the cell pointer to F16.

9. Pick Edit from the menu bar, followed by Clear. If you are using the keyboard, press Alt-EE.

These different techniques all have the same effect: they erase the contents of the highlighted cells. If you use any of these methods after highlighting a range, the contents of the range will be erased.

For a nice finishing touch to the worksheet, try using the copying techniques you learned in this step to extend the lines in rows 7 and 14 one additional column to the right. When you are finished, the worksheet should look like the worksheet in Figure 8.2.

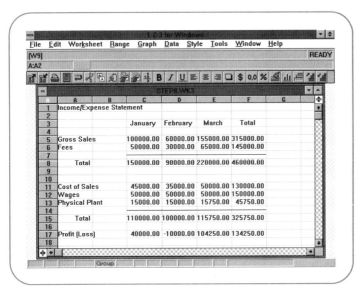

Figure 8.2: The Income/Expense Statement after editing

Step 9

Managing the Display

In this step you will learn how to delete and add rows and columns to your worksheet. You will also learn how to manage the display of a single large worksheet by splitting the screen and freezing titles.

Suppose you want to change the Income/Expense Worksheet to cover six months instead of three? Using the techniques you already know, you could simply make room for the additional data by moving the data in column F three columns to the right, thus making room for April, May, and June. But there is a better way.

Deleting Rows and Columns

Before we add more data to the example worksheet, let's make the existing worksheet as compact as possible to allow more room for the additional data. The example worksheet includes one unused column, column B, and one unused row, row 10. These can be deleted, making the worksheet more compact.

To delete column B, do the following:

1. Move the cell pointer any cell in column B.

2. Pick Worksheet from the menu bar, followed by Delete. If using the keyboard, press Alt-KD. A dialog box appears.

3. Pick the Column button to indicate that you are deleting columns. If using the keyboard, press Alt-C.

4. Since you are only deleting one column and the cell pointer is located in that column, you may now delete it by pressing Enter or picking the OK button. Column B is then deleted.

After deleting column B, the data in columns C through F is moved over one column to the left, now occupying columns B through E. Change the width of column A, using techniques described in Step 4, to keep a comfortable reading space between the data in columns A and B.

The technique for deleting a row is nearly the same as that for deleting a column. Move the cell pointer to any cell in row 10, then pick Worksheet from the menu bar, followed by Delete, as before. This time, pick the Row button in the dialog box, or press Alt-R. When you press Enter, the row will be deleted, and all data below row 10 will move up one row.

Note that while you have used this technique to delete only a single column and row, it will work just as well on highlighted ranges of rows and columns. We will use highlighted ranges in the next section, in which we will insert columns and rows.

Adding Columns

1. Move the cell pointer to any cell in column E.

2. Pick Worksheet from the menu bar, followed by Insert. If using the keyboard, press Alt-KI. A dialog box appears.

3. Pick the Column button to indicate that you are inserting columns. If using the keyboard, press Alt-C.

4. Indicate the number of columns you are inserting by moving the mouse pointer to the highlighted cell, holding down the pick button, and moving the mouse pointer two columns to the right. If the columns are not visible in the window, move the pointer anyway—1-2-3 will scroll the worksheet display, allowing you to highlight the columns. If you are using the keyboard, you can achieve the same effect by pressing the → key twice, thus enlarging the cell pointer two columns to the right. When you are finished, cells in columns E, F, and G should be highlighted. It does not matter if you highlight more than one row; 1-2-3 is interested only in the number of columns. If you have used the keyboard to highlight the range, press Enter.

5. The dialog box reappears. Notice that the default range in the text box has changed to reflect the cells you have highlighted.

6. Pick the OK button, or press Enter again, and three new columns are inserted in the spreadsheet.

To see the columns that you have added, enlarge the window by picking the Maximize button (the button with the arrowhead pointing up) in the upper-right corner of the worksheet window.

Inserting new columns has an advantage over simply moving the data in column E to column H. You will notice that the ranges in the @SUM functions have been updated to include the new columns. Instead of covering rows B through D, they now cover rows B through G. If you had simply moved the columns' data, you would have had to update the functions yourself. By adding columns, you have saved yourself the trouble.

You are now ready to add a new title, plus month headings for April, May, and June to your worksheet. Remember that the other month headings are centered, so type a caret (^) before the new month names. Use the copying techniques from Step 8 to replicate lines and formulas in the new columns. When you are finished, your worksheet should look something like Figure 9.1.

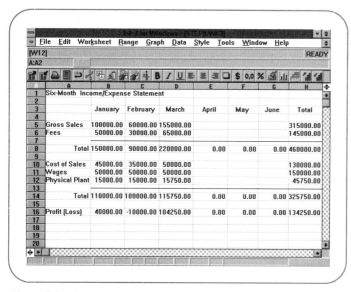

Figure 9.1: The Income/Expense Statement with new columns added

Adding Rows

Now let's add six additional expense categories to our worksheet. Our first step will be to insert some additional rows for the new categories.

1. Move the cell pointer to any cell in row 13.

2. Pick Worksheet from the menu bar, followed by Insert. If using the keyboard, press Alt-KI. A dialog box appears.

3. Pick the Row button to indicate that you are inserting rows. If using the keyboard, press Alt-R.

4. Indicate the number of rows you want to insert by moving the cell pointer to the highlighted cell, then moving the mouse pointer down five rows while holding down the pick button. If you are using the keyboard, you can achieve the same effect by pressing the ↓ key five times. When you are finished, cells in rows 13 through 18 should be highlighted. It does not matter if you highlight more than one column; 1-2-3 is interested only in the number of rows. If you have used the keyboard to highlight the range, press Enter.

5. The dialog box reappears. Notice that the default range in the text box has changed to reflect the cells you have highlighted.

6. Pick the OK button or press Enter, and six rows are inserted in the spreadsheet.

1-2-3 will do its best to update the formulas that have been moved to rows 20 and 22. You will notice that 1-2-3 correctly updated the formulas in row 22, because these formulas involved only two cell references and the change to the second reference was obvious to 1-2-3 from the location of the inserted rows. However, the formulas in row 20 are *not* updated because they use three cell addresses added together, and there is no way for 1-2-3 to be sure that you really intend for the new rows to be included in these formulas. Therefore, the formulas in row 20 must be replaced.

At this point, because of the increased number of rows involved, you would be better off replacing the simple formulas in row 20

with an @SUM function, using a range. Move the cell pointer to cell B20 and enter

`@SUM(B10..B18)`

After you enter the function, you can replicate it across columns C through G using the cell-copying techniques you have used previously. Also, be sure to replicate the formula in H12 to cells H13 through H18.

Next, you are ready to enter labels in column A for the new rows. Finally, enter new values of your choosing into the added cells. When you are finished, your worksheet should look something like the worksheet in Figure 9.2.

Whenever you add or delete rows or columns, 1-2-3 does its best to update formulas to reflect the changes you have made in the worksheet. However, if a formula anywhere in the worksheet points to a cell in a deleted row or column, the formula will become invalid and display the symbol *ERR* instead of a calculated result. When a

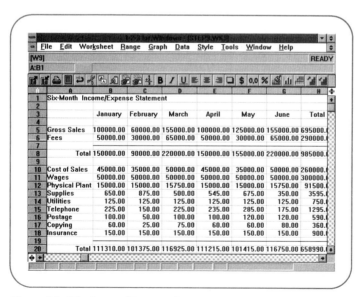

Figure 9.2: The Income/Expense Statement with new rows added

formula displays *ERR,* you must edit it to correct the problem.

1-2-3's formula-updating features are powerful, but some changes can have unpredictable effects on formulas. Whenever you make changes to the fundamental structure of your worksheet, it is worth the time to check its formulas—even those that do not display *ERR*—to make sure they are all still valid.

Splitting the Screen

As you can see, even a simple worksheet such as the example Income/Expense Statement can fill the screen, requiring you to scroll it to see all its cells. This can be difficult to manage when values in one location are related to labels or other values in a distant location. Therefore, 1-2-3 allows you to split the screen to view different parts of the spreadsheet simultaneously.

If you are using a mouse, splitting the screen is easy. For example, to split the screen so that you can view the detail rows as well as the row containing Profit/Loss data, move the mouse pointer to the double-arrow icon at the top of the vertical scroll bar, just to the right of column H. Hold the pick button down and move the mouse pointer downward on the screen. As you do so, a second window will open up on the current worksheet.

You can adjust the split window to whatever size you like. You can move the cell pointer between the two windows by moving the mouse pointer to the desired cell and pressing the pick button. The window containing the cell pointer is considered the *active window.* You can scroll to various parts of the worksheet using speed keys or the scroll bar in the active window.

To return to a single window, move the double-arrow icon back to its original position.

Notice that there is a double-arrow icon in the lower-left corner of the worksheet window as well. You can use this icon to split the screen vertically when you want to view columns in different locations side-by-side.

If you are using the keyboard, you split the window by moving the cell pointer to the row or column where you want the split and pressing Alt-WS. To split horizontally, press Alt-H; to split vertically, press Alt-V. To return to a single window, press Alt-C. Then press Enter or pick the OK button.

The worksheet in Figure 9.3 is split horizontally, and the lower window is scrolled upwards so that only the Gross Sales, Fees, Total Income, and Profit/Loss lines are visible.

When you have split the screen horizontally, you can scroll the two windows separately across rows, but when you scroll across columns, both windows move together. Likewise, when you split the screen vertically, you can scroll the windows separately across columns, but when you scroll across rows, both windows move together.

If you like, you can have the split windows move independently of each another. To do this, pick Windows from the menu bar, followed

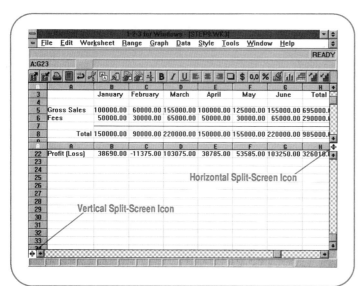

Figure 9.3: Worksheet windows split horizontally

by Split. Then, deactivate the Synchonize toggle switch, and pick the OK button. If you are using the keyboard, press Alt-WSS, followed by Enter.

Freezing Titles

You can also split the screen so that your labels in both columns and rows remain visible while you scroll though values. To see this effect on the Income/Expense Statement, move the cell pointer to cell B5 and pick Worksheet from the menu bar, followed by Titles. Then pick Both from the dialog box, and pick the OK button. If you are using the Keyboard, press Alt-KTB, followed by Enter.

At first, there may seem to be no effect, but as you move the cell pointer, you will see that the labels in column A as well as the month headings in row 3 remain on the screen and are synchronized with the movement of the cell pointer. For example, if you move the cell pointer to Cell H5, the screen will look like Figure 9.4.

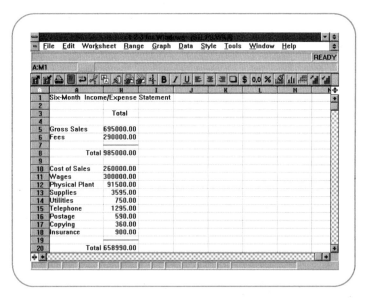

Figure 9.4: The Income/Expense Statement with frozen titles

Alternatively after picking Worksheet Titles (Alt-KT on the keyboard) and displaying the dialog box, you can freeze just those rows above the cell pointer by picking the Horizontal option (Alt-H on the keyboard), or freeze just those columns to the left of the cell pointer by picking the Vertical option (Alt-V on the keyboard). To return the worksheet to normal display, pick the Clear option (Alt-C on the keyboard). After picking your desired option, pick the OK button or press Enter.

Step 10

Utilizing Ranges

15

In previous steps, you learned basic techniques for manipulating ranges of cells. In this step you will expand on that knowledge by manipulating *named ranges.*

A named range is a group of cells that is given a unique name and treated as a unit in the worksheet. Range names make it easier to manipulate groups of cells used repeatedly in formulas, functions, and commands. Named ranges also clarify the meaning of formulas and functions that use them and make it easier to create and debug macros. (Macros will be discussed in Step 18.)

Naming ranges makes working with them easier

A range name can be up to 15 characters long, although short names are easier to manipulate and remember. You can include numbers and spaces in a range name, but do not use 1-2-3's reserved punctuation marks. Also, do not use a range name that looks like a cell address.

Naming Ranges

Let's use the Income/Expense worksheet to practice with named ranges. Suppose that you want to isolate and analyze the expenses for each month. You could use ranges for each column, creating formulas as described in previous steps. But if you have something more complex in mind, you could begin by naming the ranges for each month's expense column.

1. Move the cell pointer to cell B10.

2. Pick **Range** from the menu bar, followed by **Name**, followed by **Create**. If using the keyboard, press Alt-RNC. A dialog box appears.

3. Enter a name for the range in the Range name: text box:

    JAN

4. If the dialog box is covering up the cell range you want to name, you can move it by placing the mouse pointer in the

box's title bar, holding down the pick button, and dragging the dialog box to a new location on the screen.

5. Pick the Range text box by clicking on the cell range currently displayed in the box, highlighting the entire character string, or if using the keyboard, press Alt-A.

6. Move the mouse pointer to cell B10. Holding down the pick button, move the mouse pointer down the column, highlighting the cells from B10 through B18. Press Enter, and you have named the range.

Repeat this process for the other five columns in the expense portion of the worksheet, using the names *FEB, MAR,* and so on.

You can now use these range names in other parts of the worksheet. For example, move to cell A29 and enter the following label:

First Quarter Expenses:

Next, move the cell pointer to cell B29 and enter the following function:

`@SUM(JAN,FEB,MAR)`

Lotus 1-2-3 sums the three named ranges and displays the result in cell B29. As you can see, the meaning of this function is much clearer than it would be if it contained only a series of cell addresses.

 You can substitute a named range in any 1-2-3 command or formula that expects a cell range. You can even use a range name in response to a command prompt that expects a single cell address. If you use a range name where a single cell is expected, 1-2-3 uses the upper-left corner (the starting cell) of the range.

When a command prompt asks for a range in a worksheet that contains named ranges, 1-2-3 will display a dialog box that lists the current range names. You can pick a range name by highlighting it with the mouse pointer and then pressing Enter or picking the OK button. If you are using the keyboard, press the Tab key until the list of names is active, then highlight the name you want using the ↑ or ↓ key, and press Enter.

Naming ranges is a good habit, even if you have to spend a little extra time while building your worksheet. You will find that range names greatly simplify subsequent editing and processing of worksheets, especially as they grow larger and more complex.

Additional Range Commands

You have already been introduced to some commands that work on ranges, including **Edit Move**, **Edit Quick Copy**, **Edit Clear**, and **Range Format**. Following are some additional commands that work with ranges of cells.

Copying Formulas as Values

The **Edit Quick Copy** dialog box includes a toggle switch, Convert to values, that is useful at times when you are copying cells that contain formulas. When you activate this toggle switch, 1-2-3 copies the results of the formulas, not the formulas themselves.

Be careful when using this feature with manual recalculation. Always recalculate the worksheet *before* copying the values to avoid copying formula results that have not yet been updated.

Naming Single Cells

You can name single cells in the worksheet using labels that already exist in adjacent cells. To do so, highlight the cells containing labels and pick **Range** from the menu bar, followed by Name and Label Create. You can name the cells above, below, to the left, or to the right of the highlighted cells. This is useful in worksheets that handle long lists of data in cells adjacent to labels, because it makes the formulas consistent with the worksheet's labels. However, if you change a label later, the name of an associated cell will not change automatically. You must reinvoke this command to change the cell name. When you do change the cell name, the formulas that reference it will be updated.

Listing Current Range Names

If you like, you can create a list of all current range names and their starting cells. To make such a list, move the cell pointer to an unused area of the worksheet, then pick **R**ange from the menu bar, followed by **N**ame, followed by **P**aste Table. If you are using the keyboard, press Alt-RNP.

The program displays a dialog box indicating the range of cells where you may place the list of names, offering the active cell as the default starting cell of the range. Pick the OK button or press Enter to accept the range.

You need specify only the starting location of the range where you want the list of range names and cells to appear. Take care to use a part of the worksheet where data cannot be overwritten; try placing the list a row or two below the last data row in the worksheet. Lotus 1-2-3 copies the names into separate rows, noting the cell addresses of each range in the cell just to the right of the name. Make sure that the column holding the range names is wide enough to display the longest name.

Transposing Rows and Columns

You can reverse the orientation of rows and columns by picking **R**ange from the menu bar, followed by **T**ranspose. If using the keyboard, press Alt-RT. A dialog box appears, allowing you to enter both the source range and target cell to which you want to copy the transposed range.

It is important, when transposing ranges, that the column widths in the target area be wide enough to accommodate the transposed cells. If necessary, you can adjust the column widths after you have copied the range.

For example, use the Income/Expense Statement and move the cell pointer to cell A3. Pick **R**ange **T**ranspose, and select the range shown in Figure 10.1.

Select the text box for the destination cell, and type **M3**. Then press Enter or pick the OK button. 1-2-3 then reverses the rows and columns and writes a copy of the range starting with the destination cell. When 1-2-3 finishes copying, it returns to the cell that was active at the start of the command.

When transposing ranges, bear in mind that format changes might distort the appearance of your data. If necessary, widen any columns required to make the labels readable. Pay close attention to formatting in the target range to make sure it will accommodate the data you intend to place there. For example, you may want to change the alignment of labels using the Style Alignment command, which was described in Step 4.

Figure 10.2 illustrates the results of the transposition.

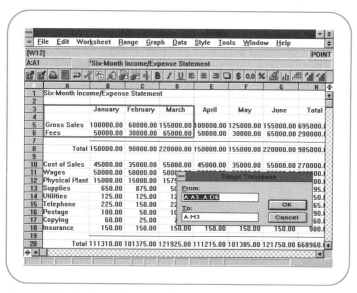

Figure 10.1: Setting up the range for the Range Transpose command

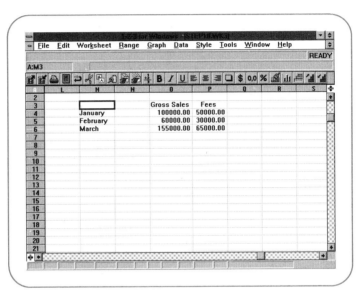

Figure 10.2: Switching rows and columns with the Range Transpose

So far, your work with files has been confined to saving and retrieving entire 1-2-3 worksheets. In this step you will learn how to save and retrieve portions of worksheets. You will also learn how to convert ASCII files into 1-2-3 files.

Saving Partial Files

Occasionally you may want to save a portion of your worksheet to a file of its own. For example, you might want to make some changes to a range of cells and store them apart from the original worksheet; or you might want to extract part of a worksheet and combine it into a completely different worksheet.

Extracting ranges

To extract the labels in column A of the Income/Expense Statement, do the following:

1. Move the cell pointer to cell A1 and highlight the range A1 through A20, using range-highlighting techniques learned in previous steps.

2. Pick File from the menu bar, followed by Extract To. A dialog box will appear.

The dialog box contains several options governing your output. If you are using a mouse, you may select any of these options in any order before picking the OK button to complete the extraction process.

To enter the name of the file to place the highlighted range in, pick the File name text box. (If you are using the keyboard, press Alt-N.) You can erase the name in this box by pressing either the backspace or delete key, assuming the name is highlighted. If you would prefer to edit the name, move the edit cursor in the box with the arrow keys, or move the mouse pointer to where you would like to make changes.

The usual text-box editing rules apply for using the keyboard. Include a subdirectory path if your intended file is not to be stored in the default.

Then press Enter to write the highlighted range to the named file.

If you include wildcard characters in the file name, you must press Enter for files matching your wild-card string to appear in the Files list box. Then you can select names from this box by picking them with the mouse pointer or by pressing Alt-F and highlighting the desired file name with the ↑ and ↓ keys. When the desired file name is highlighted, press Enter again to write the range to the file.

You can change the default subdirectory by highlighting and selecting the directories that appear in the Directories list box (if using the keyboard, press Alt-D). Likewise, you can change the default drive by activating the Drives list box (if using the keyboard, press Alt-V).

The File Extract To dialog box also contains a multiple choice list that allows you to extract the highlighted range in one of three possible formats:

- Formulas (keyboard: Alt-O) will extract formulas in the highlighted range. Labels and values are extracted in their original format.

- Values (keyboard: Alt-U) will extract values and labels in their original format, but will extract only the results of any formulas in the highlighted range.

- Text (keyboard: Alt-T) will extract the data in the highlighted range only as labels.

If you have activated this dialog box without first highlighting the range, or if you want to change the highlighted range, you may do so by highlighting the range string in the Range text box (if using a keyboard, press Alt-A) and reselecting the desired range using the mouse pointer or keyboard keys. Alternatively, you can type in the desired range.

When all extract parameters have been set, press Enter or pick the OK button with the mouse, and the data will be extracted. You can now retrieve this file as a normal 1-2-3 worksheet or combine it with any existing worksheet.

Combining Files

Any stored worksheet file or portion thereof can be combined with any currently loaded worksheet. Start by moving the cell pointer to the location in the current worksheet where you would like to paste the stored worksheet. When you combine the worksheets, 1-2-3 will place cell A1 (or the starting cell of a specified range) of the stored worksheet at this location.

Next, pick File from the menu bar, followed by Combine From. Another dialog box appears that contains File name, Files, Directory, and Drive text boxes, like those you saw when extracting files. They work the same way, except in this case you enter the name of a *source file*; that is, the file from which data will be combined with the data (if any) in the current spreadsheet.

In addition, this dialog box offers you two multiple-choice lists. The first, labeled *Action,* offers a choice of one of three options:

- Copy (Alt-C) overwrites cells in the current worksheet with cells from the source file.

- Add (Alt-A) combines values of cells in the source file that coincide with cells in the current worksheet, displaying the result.

- Subtract (Alt-S) subtracts values of cells in the source file from coinciding with cells in the current worksheet, displaying the difference.

In addition, another multiple-choice list, labeled *Source,* offers the following options:

- Entire File (Alt-E) combines the entire source file with the current worksheet.

- **R**ange: (Alt-R) combines only a portion of the stored worksheet with the current worksheet. This portion can be either a named range or range of cell addresses. You must specify the desired range in the accompanying text box.

Importing ASCII Files

You can also import information from ASCII files into the current worksheet. The file's numbers and text must be arranged in *tabular format;* that is, they must be formatted in equally spaced columns and rows and separated by tabs, commas, or spaces. Lotus 1-2-3 will import ASCII columns of numbers into adjacent worksheet columns regardless of the spacing between the columns in the ASCII file.

If your ASCII file includes both text and numbers, you must enclose the text in quotes into order to import the entire file with a single command. An example of such an ASCII file is illustrated in Figure 11.1.

To import a file such as the one shown in Figure 11.1, move the cell pointer to the location in the current worksheet where you would like the upper-left corner of the ASCII file to appear. Pick File from the menu bar, followed by Import From, followed by Numbers. If using the keyboard, press Alt-FIN.

A dialog box similar to the ones you have seen in the previous examples appears, offering you options for choosing the source file name, plus a File, Directory, and Drive list.

```
"Cost of Sales"    45000.00    35000.00        55000.00    45000.00
"Wages"            50000.00    50000.00        50000.00    50000.00
"Physical Plant"   15000.00    15000.00        15750.00    15000.00
"Supplies"           650.00      875.00          500.00      545.00
"Utilities"          125.00      125.00          125.00      125.00
"Telephone"          225.00      150.00          225.00      235.00
"Postage"            100.00       50.00          100.00      100.00
"Copying"             60.00       25.00           75.00       60.00
"Insurance"         1500.00     1500.00         1500.00     1500.00
```

Figure 11.1: An ASCII file ready for import into 1-2-3

Lotus 1-2-3 assumes a default file extension of PRN for these files and will display files with this extension in the Files list. You can enter the name of the ASCII file using any of the file-selection techniques you have learned so far.

Once the file is imported, the width of the columns may have to be adjusted to make all the data visible. Also, notice that 1-2-3 makes no assumptions about the format of numbers in the ASCII file. It will display the imported numbers in whatever value format is current. The final result of importing the file in Figure 11.1 is shown in Figure 11.2.

If your ASCII file contains text only, you can import it as a group of labels. Each line of text will be imported as a label in its own row. Surrounding quotation marks are not needed in this case.

To import ASCII text files, move the cell pointer to the desired location, pick File, followed by Import From and Text. If using the keyboard, press Alt-FIT. Then enter the name of the source file.

	A	B	C	D	E	F	G
1	Cost of Sales	45000	35000	55000	45000		
2	Wages	50000	50000	50000	50000		
3	Physical Plant	15000	15000	15750	15000		
4	Supplies	650	875	500	545		
5	Utilities	125	125	125	125		
6	Telephone	225	150	225	235		
7	Postage	100	50	100	100		
8	Copying	60	25	75	60		
9	Insurance	1500	1500	1500	1500		

Figure 11.2: The ASCII file after importing into 1-2-3

Accessing the Operating System

Managing files often involves using DOS commands to read, copy, rename, move, browse, or otherwise manipulate files on disk. With 1-2-3, you have easy access to DOS without your having to leave the program.

To access DOS from within 1-2-3, press the forward slash key, followed by **S**. The worksheet will disappear and you will see a DOS system prompt on the screen. From this prompt, you can invoke almost any DOS command. You can even invoke other applications, but be careful: when accessing DOS in this way, you have less memory available than you normally would, and memory-intensive applications may not run. Also, do not load terminate-and-stay-resident (TSR) software such as Sidekick or Prokey at this DOS prompt or you may create memory conflicts when you return to 1-2-3. Instead, load any needed TSR software before starting 1-2-3.

When you have finished using the operating system, enter

EXIT

at the DOS prompt and you will return to 1-2-3 for Windows.

Entering this last DOS command is important. *Do not restart Windows or turn off the computer from this DOS prompt.* Other programs you invoke from this DOS prompt may have serious side effects on Windows. Therefore, play it safe: use only DOS file-management commands and return promptly to 1-2-3 by invoking **EXIT**.

Step 12

Linking Spreadsheets

You have seen in previous steps how you can use formulas to reference data in different cells of the worksheet and import ranges of cells from different files on disk. In this step you will learn how to use formulas to reference cells in other worksheets. You may also include up to 256 worksheet *layers* in a single file, effectively incorporating many single-layer worksheets in the same file.

Linking allows you to consolidate data from several sources into a single worksheet. To understand linking, imagine that you had a copy of the Income/Expense statement for several outlets of a store, each named with the letters *OUTLET* plus a number: OUTLET1.WK3, OUTLET2.WK3, and so on. Now suppose that you needed a summary of the outlet information in a single worksheet. You have two ways to accomplish this:

Linking consolidates worksheets

- If you needed to maintain your outlet information in separate disk *files,* you could link cells from these disk files into a consolidating worksheet.

- If you prefered, you could maintain your outlet and summary information in the same disk file by creating a worksheet *layer* for each outlet, plus a separate layer for the consolidated report. This method makes use of a *3-D worksheet.*

Creating File-Linking Formulas

A *file-linking formula* is one that refers to a cell (or a named range) in another worksheet. You create the reference by including the name of the referenced worksheet (called the *source worksheet*) between a set of double angle brackets in the formula. The worksheet that the formula resides in is called the *target worksheet.* It is updated to include the contents of the referenced file's cells each time the target worksheet is loaded.

If the drive and subdirectory path of the source worksheet are not the same as for the target worksheet, you must include the drive and path in the source file's name.

The following formula refers to cell C5 in the file OUTLET1.

`+<<C:\123W\OUTLET1>>C5`

Notice how the file name and its path location are enclosed in a pair of angle brackets. The name within these brackets must always reference an accessible worksheet.

Using Range Names in Linking Formulas

You can use a range name instead of a cell address if you want the formula to reference the starting cell of the entire range.

Using range names is a good idea. When you use range names to link cells in other worksheets, you can make changes to those worksheets, such as moving data or inserting rows or columns, and the named ranges will be updated automatically. Since, in the target worksheet, you referenced a range name instead of a cell address, the target worksheet will remain accurate.

Creating a Sample Summary Worksheet

The following example demonstrates a simple consolidation. Figures 12.1 and 12.2 illustrate Income/Expense Statements for two different outlets. You can create these worksheets using commands you have learned so far.

As you create these worksheets, notice that the global format is fixed, two decimal places. Each outlet's first- and second-quarter income and expenses are summarized using formulas that reference the appropriate cells in the worksheet. The summary of income and expense totals, by quarter, is listed in cells A18 through G19.

These two source worksheets are named *OUTLET1* and *OUTLET2*. You can link these two worksheets to a target worksheet called

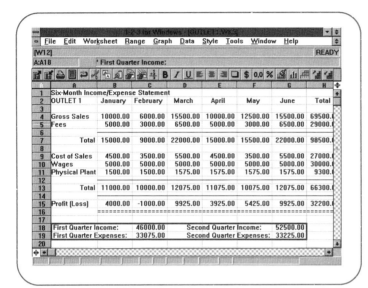

Figure 12.1: Sample worksheet for Outlet 1

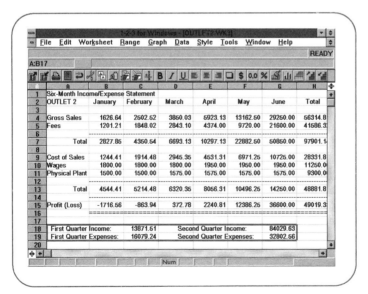

Figure 12.2: Sample worksheet for Outlet 2

SUMMARY using the following steps:

1. Close all current worksheets using the **File Close** commands and open a new worksheet using **File Open**.

2. If necessary, change the column widths in the new worksheet to match the dimensions of the source worksheets.

3. Enter labels indicating that the worksheet is a summary of Outlets 1 and 2, as shown in Figure 12.3.

4. Place the following formula in cell A5:

   `+<<OUTLET1>>A18`

   Notice that the label from the OUTLET1 worksheet is now repeated in cell A6 of the current worksheet. This is the starting cell of the named range.

5. Use the cell-copying techniques you have learned to replicate this formula throughout the range A5 through G6. Once you replicate the formula in cell A5, the entire

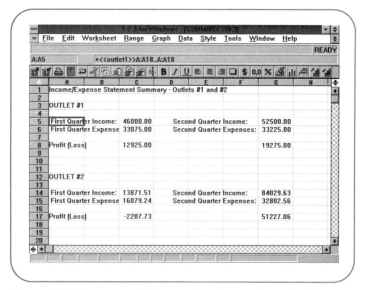

Figure 12.3: Summary worksheet—cleaned up and completed

named range will be referenced in the current worksheet.

6. The zeros that appear in the target worksheet are the result of your having replicated the formula throughout cells A5 through G6 in the target worksheet. Since you do not need all these copies, you can clean up the result by highlighting the cells containing the zeros and pressing the Delete key.

7. Repeat steps 4, 5, and 6. Reference the named range from the OUTLET2 worksheet, place it in cell A12, copy it in cells A12 through G13, and clean up the extra formulas in columns B, E, and F.

8. Add standard formulas for subtracting expenses from income to determine profit and loss. When you are finished, the result should look like Figure 12.3.

The advantage of linking these worksheets can be seen if you save this summary worksheet and reload either OUTLET1 or OUTLET2. Make changes to update the first- and second-quarter totals, then save the outlet worksheet and reload the summary worksheet. All the changes that you made at the outlet level are reflected in the summary worksheet.

Nesting Linked Files

You can link a worksheet to other worksheets, which in turn are linked to still other worksheets, and you can nest linked worksheets as many levels deep as you require. For example, your outlet worksheets might be linked to a regional summary, which is in turn linked to a national summary.

When manipulating complex systems of linked worksheets, you must pay very close attention to updating every worksheet involved in any given transaction. A linked formula will only retrieve the information available in the source worksheet at the time the source worksheet was last saved.

In other words, after changing a worksheet, retrieve and save any linked worksheets that reference it, all the way up through the chain, to insure the complete accuracy of your information.

Creating a 3-D Worksheet

If you prefer, you can include your summary and outlet information in a single worksheet file. To do this you must first create additional layers, one for each outlet, below the first worksheet layer, which will contain the consolidation information.

You can create a 3-D worksheet based on the data in the worksheets you have just created, using the following steps:

1. Open the summary worksheet you created in the previous sequence and erase the cells containing linking formulas, but not the labels or the Profit/Loss formulas.

2. Create two additional worksheet layers by picking Worksheet from the menu bar, followed by Insert. Pick Sheet from the multiple-choice box, and indicate 2 in the Quantity: text box. Then pick the OK button. If you are using the keyboard, press Alt-KISQ, followed by **2** and Enter.

3. Layer B, a blank worksheet layer, now appears on the screen. Pick File from the menu bar, followed by Combine From, and select OUTLET1.WK3 from the file-name list in the dialog box. Then pick the OK button. If you are using the keyboard, press Alt-FB, then highlight the file name using the ↑ or ↓ keys, then press Enter.

4. Shift to layer C by pressing Ctrl-Page Up. Again, pick File Combine From, followed this time by OUTLET2.WK3. Then press Enter.

5. Shift to layer A by pressing Ctrl-Page Down *twice*. The original summary worksheet will now be visible.

6. Move the cell pointer to A5 and enter:

   `+B:A18`

7. Use the copying techniques you have already learned to replicate this formula in the ranges A5..A6, C5..D6, and G5..G6.

8. Move the cell pointer to A12 and enter:

   +C:A18

9. Replicate this formula in the ranges A12..A13, C12..D13, and G12..G13.

10. Finally, to see all three layers on the screen together, pick Windows from the menu bar, followed by Split. Pick Perspective from the multiple-choice list, then pick the OK button. If you are using the keyboard, press Alt-WSP followed by Enter.

11. Press the Home key, and your screen should look like Figure 12.4.

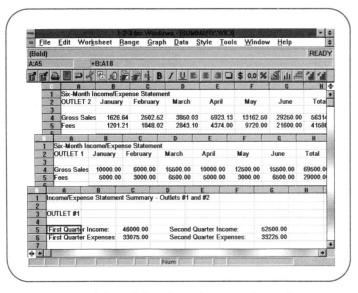

Figure 12.4: Multiple worksheet layers in perspective mode

Printing Spreadsheets

Lotus 1-2-3 offers two options for printing worksheets: you can print to a hard-copy printing device such as a dot-matrix or laser printer, or you can print to a file. Both printing options provide you with a wide variety of settings that control the format of the output. You will learn about fundamental printing options in this step.

Output to Printer

To send your output to a printer, first highlight the range of cells you want to print. Then pick File from the menu bar, followed by Print. If you are using the keyboard, press Alt-FP. This will display a dialog box entitled File Print. This box will indicate the current printer configuration and includes a text box that indicates the range of cells to be printed (currently matching the range you have highlighted).

You can relocate the File Print dialog box on the screen by moving the mouse pointer to the title bar, holding down the mouse button and moving the pointer to another part of the screen. This is useful if you want to change the indicated range of cells and the dialog box is covering the starting cell.

Other text boxes in the File Print dialog box control various rudimentary aspects of printing:

- From page: Use this box to indicate what page number you would like to begin printing at if your highlighted range spans multiple printed pages. Default is page 1.

- To: Use this box, also in case of multiple-page printouts, to indicate at what page number you would like to stop printing. If the page number indicated here is higher than the last printed page of the range, all pages will be printed and the higher numbers ignored. Default is page 9999.

- Starting page number: Use this box in cases where page numbers are to be printed on the hard copy and you want to begin printing with a specific page number; this is useful when the printout will be inserted in a larger report. Default is Page 1.

This dialog box includes an OK button to begin the printing process, and a Cancel button to abort and return to the worksheet.

In addition to these options, this dialog box also includes buttons labeled Preview and Page Setup.

Pick the Preview button (or press Alt-V) to display an approximation of the final printout on the screen. This feature is a great convenience, especially when printing highly formatted worksheets, as it can help you spot and correct printing setup errors before initiating the actual printing process. Press any key to step through the display of each printed page. If you press Esc, you will return to the worksheet.

The Page Setup button opens a second dialog box, entitled File Page Setup. Both of these dialog boxes are shown in Figure 13.1.

The File Page Setup dialog box allows you to pick and choose from among a variety of printing options:

- Header: Enter any text you would like included at the top of each page. Leave this box blank for a blank top margin. If you include a header, be sure to use a top margin wide enough to accommodate the header and enough space to separate the header string from the worksheet data.

- Footer: Enter any text to be included at the bottom of each page, or leave blank. As with headers, be sure to adjust the bottom-margin setting so that you have a reasonable amount of space between the worksheet data and the footer.

Other text boxes allow you to select repeating column and row *borders* for your printout (this is the printing equivalent of freezing titles):

- Columns: Indicate a range of columns to be repeated as a border on the left of each printed page. For example, if

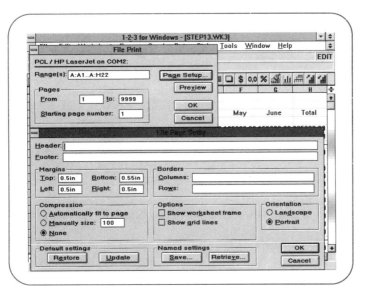

Figure 13.1: The File Print and File Page Setup dialog boxes

you are printing a wide worksheet that must be printed on several pages, and column A contains identifying labels for each row, you might want to repeat these labels on each page, to clarify the association with their respective values.

• Rows: As with columns, you can indicate a range of rows that you would like to use as a top border on each page for the sake of clarity.

If you use border columns or rows, do not include them in the printing range. Otherwise, they will be repeated in the printout.

Four text boxes control the size of the printed margins, either in inches, millimeters, or lines/characters, depending on your printer's capabilities: Top, Bottom, Left, and Right, each indicating the size of their respective margins.

If your printer has graphics capability and is capable of scaling the size of printouts, you may choose one of three *compression* modes that control the amount of data on a single page:

- Automatically fit to page: Select this option to compress the printout to the extent necessary to fit the range on a page.

- Manually size: Select this option to indicate compression by a *percentage factor* that you enter in the accompanying text box; where *100* indicates full size, *50* indicates half size, and so forth.

- None: Select this option to disable all compression. The worksheet will be printed full-size. This is the default.

Various toggle switches allow you to enable or disable certain printing options:

- Show formulas: Enable this switch to print the formulas in the worksheet. Disable to print formula results.

- Show worksheet frame: Enable this switch to include column letters and row numbers in the printout. Disable to print without column and row identifiers.

- Show grid lines: Enable this switch to print lines between the worksheet's cells. Disable to print without lines.

If your printer can print sideways (landscape), pick the Landscape multiple-choice button, or pick the Portrait multiple-choice button to print upright on the page.

Other buttons in this window allow you to control and simplify the setup process:

- Restore: Pick this button to return the print settings to their default values.

- Update: Pick this button to save the current settings as the new default.

- Save: Pick this button to store the current printing setup for later recall.

- Retrieve: Pick this button to display a list of named printing setups, which you may select using the mouse pointer or arrow keys, as described in previous steps.

When the print settings are acceptable, pick the OK button or press Enter. To abort the setup process, pick the Cancel button. If you are using the keyboard and want to cancel, highlight the Cancel button using the Tab key, then press Enter, or press Esc. (Depending on the location of the screen cursor, you may have to press Esc twice.)

To start the output to the printer, pick the OK button in the File Print dialog box. If you are using the keyboard, highlight the button if necessary by pressing the Tab key, then press Enter.

You can cancel a printout by pressing the Cancel button that appears on the screen during printing, or by pressing Ctrl-Break. However, the printer may not stop printing immediately. Many printers hold a large amount of data in an internal *buffer,* and this data will continue to print. Refer to your printer's documentation for help in clearing its internal buffer.

Tips on Printing

1-2-3 allows you considerable power and flexibility when printing. As you gain experience with 1-2-3, you will enjoy its flexibility; but for the beginner, 1-2-3's many options can be quite confusing. You can minimize your problems if you take time in advance to calculate the size of the paper you are using in terms of vertical lines-per-inch and horizontal characters-per-inch. Then set your 1-2-3 margin defaults to reflect your printer's capabilities.

Also, be sure you know the *printing width* of your selected range. The printing width is the total of the widths of all the columns in the range. To fit the columns on one page, set 1-2-3's right margin to the printing width plus the left-margin setting, and be sure that your printer can print with these settings.

If you cannot fit all the columns in your selected range within the margin settings, 1-2-3 will print the extra columns on separate pages. This is true for both printed output and disk files. If you like, you can adjust your margin settings so that 1-2-3 will break the columns in a logical way. If you set your margins this way, it is usually a good idea to set column borders, using File Print Page Setup, to repeat the identifying labels in your worksheet.

When highlighting a range that includes labels that overlap cells, be sure to highlight all of the text you intend to print, not just the cells that contain the labels. If text is only partially highlighted, it may appear truncated in the printout.

Make liberal use of the Preview feature. It saves both time and paper when printing a complicated worksheet.

Printer Setup

When printing worksheets, 1-2-3 accesses the printing features already built into Windows. Pick File from the menu bar, followed by Printer Setup. This displays the File Printer Setup dialog box, which includes a list of available printer drivers that have been installed using Windows. If you have installed more than one printer driver under Windows, you can pick a driver from this list using the mouse pointer. If you are using the keyboard, press Alt-P and highlight the printer driver using the ↑ or ↓ key, then press Enter.

This dialog box also includes a button labeled Setup. Pick this button (or press Alt-S) to access the currently selected Windows printer driver. Printer features vary widely among different devices, and the appearance of this dialog box will depend on the available features of your chosen printer. You can adjust the default features for your printer using the standard Windows techniques for picking options from lists, toggle switches, and buttons. Consult your printer documentation for more information on your printer's available configuration options and their effect on the final printout.

When you have made your setup choices, pick the OK button, or highlight this button and press Enter. To cancel the setup process, pick the Cancel button, or press Esc.

Output to a File

When you print to a file instead of the printer, you create an ASCII file that represents the printed output of the worksheet in a file on disk. This file can be copied and moved to another computer, sent to a printing device with DOS commands, or modified with other software such as word processors or advanced page-formatting programs.

To print to a text file, choose File from the menu bar, followed by Extract to. The File Extract To dialog box appears, containing text and list boxes (for file names, directories, and drives) that work exactly like those you have seen earlier.

This dialog box also offers you a multiple-choice list that determines the content and format of the output file:

- Formulas: Select this option to create a worksheet file that includes the actual formulas in the highlighted range, rather than their results.

- Values: Select this option to create a worksheet file that includes the results of formulas in the highlighted range, rather then the formulas themselves.

- Text: Select this option to create an ASCII text file of the highlighted data. Normally, this text file will include the results of formulas. If you want the actual formulas in your ASCII file, first reformat the cells containing for- mulas. Use Text format, so that the formulas are displayed on the screen.

When printing to a file, columns that are wide enough to display labels and values on the screen may not be wide enough to print data properly, even when all the text and values have been highlighted. If your labels appear truncated in the output, or some numbers in the ASCII file appear as asterisks, make your worksheet columns wide enough to accommodate the full contents of the cells, and try again.

It is sometimes difficult to grasp the relationships between sets of data when the data is presented as a series of numbers in columns. Lotus 1-2-3 allows you to represent data visually in the form of *graphs*, which you can create quickly and easily from your worksheets. In this step, you will learn how to create several types of graphs.

Selecting the Best Graph Type

1-2-3 offers you a choice of the following types of graphs:

- Line: Represents data as a line connecting points. Each point represents a value in the worksheet. The graph can contain as many as six lines. Line graphs are useful for measuring changes in values over time.

- Area: Again represents data using lines, but with the area below each line filled in. Area graphs display changes in several sets of values over time, representing the relationship between the different value sets and the total.

- Bar: Represents data as a group of bars, each representing a value in the worksheet. The graph can contain as many as six sets of bars, with up to 200 bars per set. Bar graphs are useful for comparing related individual values.

- XY: Represents at least two data series as a line connecting a series of symbols. You can compare up to six data series relative to a single data series. XY graphs are useful for representing relationships among values that are dependent upon other values.

- Stack-Bar: Represents data as a series of bars stacked vertically. Each stacked bar is the sum of discrete parts. This graph is useful when comparing subtotals along with totals.

- Pie: Represents a series of values as a portion of a circle, or pie. You can include one data series in the pie. This graph is useful for representing the relationship between a whole and its parts.

- HLCO: HLCO graphs are used to chart fluctuations in data such as stock prices. They have four data ranges: high, low, open, and close. The high and low data points (usually the high and low prices for a given time period) are connected to form a vertical line. The opening price is a horizontal line extending to the left of the vertical line; the closing price is a horizontal line extending to the right.

- Mixed: Mixed graphs are combined bar and line graphs; these graphs are useful when comparing changes between individual values over time. Mixed graphs can include up to three sets of bars and three lines in the same graph.

Drawing a Line Graph

To experiment with 1-2-3's graphing features, use the example Income/Expense Statement shown in Figure 14.1. For clarity, the global format in this worksheet is Comma, with zero decimal places.

You will create two graphs: a line and a bar graph. The line graph will represent profitability during the period from January to June. The bar graph will compare gross income to expenses for each month during that period.

To create the line graph, pick Graph from the menu bar, followed by New. A dialog box appears, which you use to enter the name of the graph and the range of data it represents. Enter a graph name of your choosing or accept the default name, *GRAPH1*. Since you will enter the data ranges for this graph using subsequent menu commands, you can accept whatever default data range is offered here. When you pick the OK button, a graph will be displayed. It is not necessary that the graph be meaningful at this point.

After you have given a name to your new graph, you must select a graph type (if it is not a line graph already) and the ranges of data to be included.

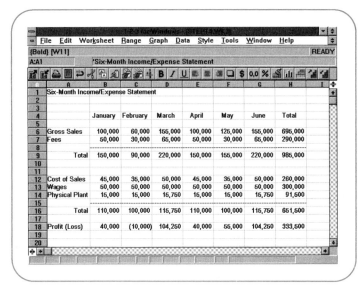

Figure 14.1: Sample worksheet to use for graphing

To check the graph type, pick Chart from the menu bar, followed by Type. A dialog box displays a lengthy list of graph types. You can select one by picking the button to its left or, if using the keyboard, by pressing the underlined letter in its name. For example, to select the Line graph, pick the button to the left of Line, or press **L**.

After you have selected Line graph, pick the OK button or press Enter.

The next step is to enter the specific ranges of data that you would like to graph. To enter the data ranges, pick Chart from the menu bar, followed by Ranges. The Chart Ranges dialog box appears, as pictured in Figure 14.2. You will use this dialog box to enter two data ranges: the **X** data range and A range.

Highlight the current **X** data range, if any is showing, by picking it with the mouse pointer or, if using the keyboard, by pressing Alt-**X**. Enter the range B4 through G4 for the **X** data range.

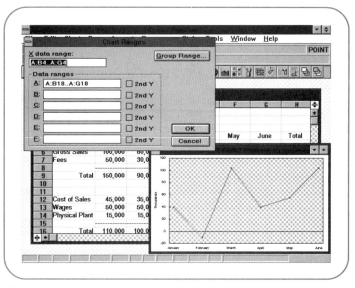

Figure 14.2: The Chart Ranges dialog box, along with the basic line graph

Next, select the A range text box and enter the range B18 through G18, the difference between income and expenses for the period. If other ranges appear in the Chart Ranges dialog box, delete them by highlighting them and pressing the Delete key.

To view the line graph, pick the OK button or, if using the keyboard, by highlighting the button with the Tab key and pressing Enter.

A graph should appear like the one shown back in Figure 14.2.

You can save this graph as part of the worksheet by pressing the control menu box in the upper-left corner of the graph's window, followed by Close. If you are using the keyboard, hold down the control key and press F4. Of course, if you don't save your changes to the worksheet, the graph will be lost.

Drawing a Bar Graph

To create a bar graph, pick Graph from the menu bar, followed by New, as before. After naming the graph or accepting the default, *GRAPH2*, pick the OK button. Next indicate the graph type by picking Chart, Type, and Bar from the dialog box, followed by OK.

As before, pick Chart Ranges to indicate the ranges of data for the graph. For the **X** data range, use B4 through G4, the month headings in the worksheet. For the **A** data range, enter the range B9 through G9. This line shows the total income for each month in the sample worksheet. For the **B** range, enter B16 through G16. This line shows the expenditures for the same period. When you pick the OK button, you should see a bar graph something like the one illustrated in Figure 14.3.

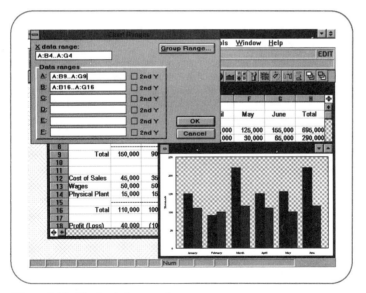

Figure 14.3: The basic bar graph

Graphs are saved with a worksheet when you name them, so you should save your worksheets often when creating and updating graphs to ensure that you do not lose a graph you are working on.

Adding Labels and Numbers

Once you have established the basic visual information in your graph, you can enhance its appearance by adding descriptive labels such as titles and legends. You can add labels, titles, and other descriptive enhancements to any graph.

To add a title to your bar graph:

1. Pick Graph from the menu bar, followed by View, and select the bar graph, GRAPH2, from the Graph View dialog box. Then pick the OK button or press Enter. The bar graph will be displayed on your screen.

2. Pick Chart from the graph menu bar, followed by Headings. In the Chart Headings dialog box, you can enter the following descriptive text for your graph:

   • Title: This is the main title, which by default is centered at the top of the graph.

   • Subtitle: This text appears below the main title.

   • Note: This text appears in the lower-left corner of the graph.

   • 2nd note: This text appears below the note text.

3. Enter the following in the Title text box:

   `Income & Expenses - First 6 Months`

   and pick the OK button or press Enter.

After you press Enter, 1-2-3 displays the graph with the title added.

To add legends:

1. Pick Chart from the graph menu bar, followed by Legend. The Chart Legend dialog box pops up.

2. Pick the **A** range and enter

   Income

3. Pick the **B** range and enter

   Expenses

4. Pick the OK button or press Enter to redisplay the graph with the legends added.

You can add labels to the *X* and *Y* axes of this graph as well. For example, to add a label to the *Y* axis, pick Chart from the menu bar, followed by Axis and **Y**. This displays the Chart Axis Y dialog box. Pick the **O**ptions button in this dialog box, which displays another dialog box. In the Axis Title text box, enter

U.S. Dollars

Then pick the OK button, followed by the OK button in the Chart Axis Y dialog box, to redisplay the graph.

You might find the graph easier to read if you were to extend horizontal lines from the values along the *Y* axis. To do this, pick Chart from the menu bar, followed by Borders/Grids. The Chart Borders/Grids dialog box appears. Pick the *Y-axis* toggle switch, then pick the OK button or press Enter. Last, pick the OK button in the Chart Borders/Grids dialog box, and 1-2-3 redisplays the graph with axis lines added.

Finally, you may want to maximize the graph window on screen, in order to make the added text easier to view. If you have made all the above enhancements, the graph should look like Figure 14.4. Remember to save the worksheet, which also saves the named graph.

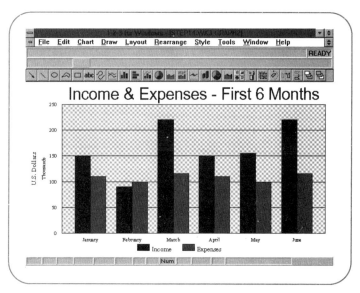

Figure 14.4: The basic bar graph with enhancements

When you want to return to the worksheet, repeatedly press Ctrl-Tab to cycle through the open windows until the worksheet window is highlighted. You can also resize or close the graph window using standard Windows commands.

Before you create a graph using real-world data, take a moment to think about the relationships you want to express. Select the graph type that will convey your message most clearly and quickly. For best results, keep your graphs simple and uncluttered. Once you have established the correct graph type and selected the data to include, don't hesitate to experiment, saving the graphs you like best for later recall. You cannot "hurt" 1-2-3 or your data by trying out several options.

Step 15

Enhancing Graphs

The fundamental techniques for producing 1-2-3 graphs yield effective general-purpose graphs, but 1-2-3 includes additional commands and features that allow you to customize these graphs and give them more punch. Graphs can be enhanced with text, lines, curves, arrows, and polygons, all of which are known as *graphic objects*. In addition, you can make numerous changes to the appearance of the information in the basic graph.

Enhancing a Line Graph

For example, consider the line graph you produced in the previous step. In its current format, it is accurate, but you can add information to increase its impact. This step will show you how to add information such as the name of the business and the exact earnings figures for each month, as well as how to modify the graph itself.

Graphs are enhanced to amplify their meaning

To retrieve the Line graph, open the example worksheet and pick Graph from the menu bar, followed by View; then pick the line-graph name from the dialog box on screen. This opens a new window, containing the line graph, as illustrated in the previous step in Figure 14.2.

To make the upcoming changes more readable on the screen, enlarge the graph window by picking the Maximize button (the one with the small arrowhead pointing upward) in the upper-right corner of the window. If you are using the keyboard, you can enlarge the window by pressing Alt-F and the ← key twice, and then picking Maximize from the graph window's control menu.

To add text to the graph, pick Draw from the menu bar, followed by Text. In the Draw Text dialog box, enter a company name, for example:

```
Roscoe's Fish Farm
```

When you have typed in the desired text, press Enter or pick the OK button.

At this point, you can move the text anywhere in the graph window with the mouse pointer or arrow keys. Do not be concerned with the size of the text at this point; you will have an opportunity to change it soon. In this example, place the text near the upper-left corner of the graph. When the text is in position, press the pick button or Enter.

Notice that the text is surrounded with small squares. These squares indicate that this current object is *selected* and may be edited. We will edit this text by changing its size.

Objects must be selected before you can edit them

To change the size of the selected text, pick Style from the menu bar, followed by Font. Lotus 1-2-3 displays a list of available text fonts. In this case, pick ArialMT, using the mouse pointer or the arrow keys. Press Enter, and 1-2-3 adjusts the text size.

You can repeat this sequence of steps to add whatever text you like to make the graph more meaningful. The example graph in this step adds the exact earnings amount (income minus expenses) for each month at appropriate points along the graph line, along with the amount of total earnings ($333,500). As you add this text, you can adjust the position, font, and size to create a pleasing and balanced effect.

If you find it necessary to move the text again after changing its appearance, you can select the text with the mouse pointer. Then hold down the pick button and move the text to the new location.

If you are using the keyboard, you can select objects by pressing Alt-E, followed by Alt-SC. (This is the same as picking Edit, Select, and Cycle from the screen menus.) When the dialog box appears, press Alt-N (the Next button) to cycle through the objects until the one you want is highlighted, then change its appearance using the menu commands. You can move objects only with the mouse.

To select more than one object, hold down the Shift key as you pick each one.

For example, imagine that the earnings for the month of March were deserving of some special notice. Say, for instance, that these earnings were a single-month record high. If you like, you could highlight this fact by drawing attention to the March earnings with additional text and an arrow pointing to the portion of the graph that represents them.

To add an arrow to the graph, pick **Draw** from the menu bar, followed by **Arrow**. Use the mouse or arrow keys to move the cursor to where the end point of the arrow should be. Select this point with the pick button or press the spacebar. Then, move the cursor to where the next point on the arrow should be. To draw the arrowhead, press Enter instead of picking the last point.

To draw a circle or ellipse in a graph, pick **Draw** followed by **Ellipse**. Move the cursor to one corner of an imaginary rectangle that will enclose the circle or ellipse. Pick this point, or press the spacebar. Move the cursor to the opposite corner of this imaginary rectangle and pick that point or press Enter. Lotus 1-2-3 then draws the circle or ellipse within the rectangle.

Drawing circles and ellipses

You can draw other objects by following the same technique; that is, you create the object by defining points in the graph window. Feel free to experiment by drawing other objects.

To get rid of an object, select it and press the Delete key. To restore the last deleted object, press the Ins key.

Enhancing the Chart

For editing and enhancement purposes, notice that 1-2-3 refers to the basic graph as the *chart*. You can make a number of enhancements to the basic graph by picking **Chart** from the menu bar, followed by that portion of the basic graph that you would like to change.

For example, the current Y-axis of the example line graph is not particularly informative. To enhance the Y-axis, pick **Chart** followed by **Axis** and **Y** (or press Alt-CXY). When the dialog box appears, pick the **O**ptions button (Alt-O). A second dialog box appears. In the Axis title text box, enter:

    Dollars U.S.

Next, pick Manual from the multiple choice list. This eliminates 1-2-3's standard Y-axis text. Then, pick the OK button or press Enter.

In the first dialog box, pick the Format button. This displays a dialog box containing standard 1-2-3 value formats. Pick the comma format using the mouse or arrow keys and indicate zero decimal places in the text box. Then pick the OK button or press Enter.

Finally, pick Manual from the Axis units multiple-choice list in the first dialog box, and enter 0 in the Exponent text box. Pick the OK button or press Enter, and the Y-axis enhancements are added to the graph.

When you have added the various enhancements described here, the line graph will look something like the line graph pictured in Figure 15.1.

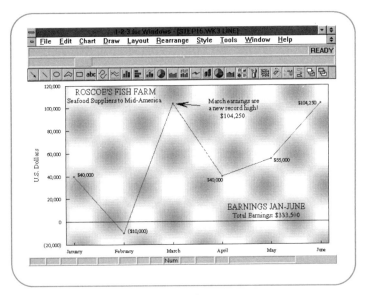

Figure 15.1: The enhanced line graph

Saving the Graph

If you want to print the graph using 1-2-3, you must add it to a range of cells in the worksheet. This technique is described in detail in Step 19.

You can save the graph as a *bitmap* file by first copying it to the Windows clipboard and then moving it from the clipboard into any Windows program (for example, the Windows Paint program) that can edit and print bitmap files.

To copy the graph to the clipboard, make the graph window the current window, then pick Edit from the menu bar, followed by Copy. You must copy the entire graph to the clipboard; you do not have the option of copying portions of the graph, although you can further edit the bitmap file in Windows' Paint or a similar program.

To bring the bitmap file into the other Windows application, start the application and invoke the Edit Paste command. Do this before invoking any other commands that may change the contents of the clipboard. Once the graph has been captured in this way, you may use the other application to print it or make additional changes as you see fit.

Step 16

Creating a Database

15

A database is a thoughtfully organized collection of related pieces of information. In this step, you will learn how to create a 1-2-3 database, using the 1-2-3 worksheet tools you have learned so far (entering data in cells, moving and copying ranges, inserting and deleting rows and columns, and so forth).

Database Structure

Databases organize data into units called *records*. Each record is divided into *fields* that separate the record's contents into general categories. The field structure of a database applies to all records in that database. This guarantees that the order of the fields will be consistent and that each field will hold the same type of data.

Records and fields

Because 1-2-3 uses fields to sort and search the database, it is important that 1-2-3 be able to differentiate between them. Thus, each field in the database is given a unique identifying name.

For example, in a marketing list, each record would contain data on a single customer and might be broken down into fields for the customer's first name, last name, street address, city, state, zip code, and income bracket. This field structure would be repeated for each record in the list.

Lotus 1-2-3's basic worksheet structure of rows and columns is well suited for organizing data into records and fields. Each row in the database represents a record, and each column represents a field.

The theoretical maximum number of records you may have in a 1-2-3 database is 8192, because this is the maximum number of rows in the worksheet. The maximum number of fields is 256, because this is the maximum number of columns in the worksheet. In practice, your databases will probably be smaller.

The allowable size for databases is governed by the amount of memory you have. Like any 1-2-3 worksheet, an entire database

Database size

must be in RAM to function. You can increase the maximum limit on records in your database by adding additional memory to your computer, thus allowing larger worksheets to be loaded into RAM.

In most cases, it makes sense to maintain a database in its own file. You can create a database that is part of a larger worksheet, but if you do so, be sure to store it in a relatively remote area of the worksheet or on a separate worksheet layer, so that it is not affected by changes you make to the rest of the worksheet. Likewise, you wouldn't want changes you made to your database to affect the rest of the worksheet.

Defining the Database

Before setting up your 1-2-3 database, think carefully about what kinds of information you want to extract from it; knowing in advance what kinds of reports you want to generate will help you design an efficient and useful database.

For example, if you wanted to create a customer list for marketing purposes, you would want your database to include names, mailing addresses, and perhaps information about annual incomes. If you wanted to use this database to create lists targeted to individuals of a particular income living in certain areas of the country, you would need to keep the mailing addresses and income information in separate fields, so you could sort and search the database based on those fields. If you wanted to sort the names alphabetically, it would also be important to create separate fields for last names and first names.

Figure 16.1 shows what such a database might look like. Notice that the field names appear in columns just above the database's data. The names must be listed in a single row just above the data. Although 1-2-3 uses only one row for field names, you can add additional explanatory text above the field names for the sake of clarity.

Go ahead and enter the data shown in Figure 16.1. Use the same techniques you use to enter data in a standard worksheet. Notice that the normal formatting codes you have learned so far also apply to

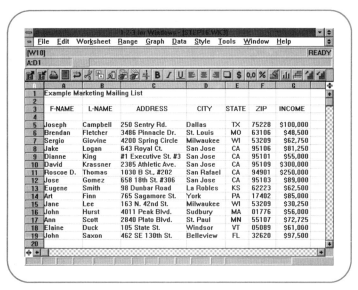

Figure 16.1: A simple marketing list

fields in this database. The only numeric data in the database is the annual-income data; all other entries should be treated as labels and will not be subject to any calculations.

To keep the database structure clear, you should enlarge each column's width so that the longest item appears entirely within its column. You can insert blank columns into a database for the sake of appearance, but you should not include blank rows as these will disrupt sorting and searching.

Adding and Deleting Records

Once you have set the structure of your database, it will be easy to maintain. You can insert new records into the database by positioning the cell pointer at the appropriate row, picking Worksheet from the menu bar, followed by Insert, then indicating Row in the Worksheet Insert dialog box. If using the keyboard, press Alt-KIR. Pick the OK button or press Enter to add space for the new record.

You can delete records from your database by moving the cell pointer to a field in the unwanted record, picking Worksheet from the menu bar, followed by **Delete**, and indicating **R**ow in the Worksheet Delete dialog box. If using the keyboard, press Alt-KDR. To delete the row, pick the OK button or press Enter.

Naming Field Ranges

You will find that you can manipulate the database more easily if you give your database columns range names that match the field names. For example, in Figure 16.1, you can identify the column containing last names as a range, giving it the same range name as the field name, *L-NAME*.

1. Using the cell pointer, highlight the range B5..B19.

2. Pick **R**ange from the menu bar, followed by **N**ame, followed by **C**reate.

3. In the Range Name Create dialog box, pick the **R**ange name: text box (keyboard: Alt-R), and enter **L-NAME**. This sequence is illustrated in Figure 16.2.

4. After you have indicated the range name, pick the OK button or press Enter.

Notice that the field-name cell is not included in the named range, because you do not want it included in any subsequent sorting and searching you do in the database.

You can use this technique to name all the other columns in the example database.

Importing Data

Before importing or combining any files in 1-2-3, save the file using the **F**ile **S**ave or File Save As commands. That way, if something goes wrong, you can easily retrieve the original file.

You can import data from other Windows programs into your 1-2-3 database, provided both programs support Windows' Dynamic Data Exchange feature.

For example, suppose you wanted to bring data from an external database into your worksheet.

1. Begin by starting the external database and opening the source datafile.

2. Pick Edit Copy from the database's menu, and copy the desired records to the Windows clipboard.

3. Return to 1-2-3 and load the worksheet that will receive the data.

4. Highlight a range of cells large enough to receive the information from the clipboard.

5. Pick Edit from the menu bar, followed by Paste, to add the data from the clipboard to your worksheet.

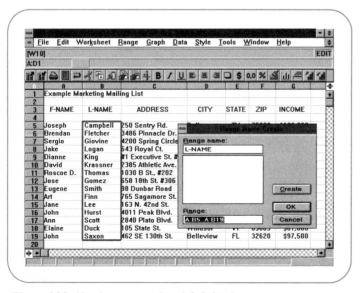

Figure 16.2: Naming a range in a 1-2-3 database

This type of data exchange relies on structural compatibility between the records and fields in both files. In other words, the fields
should be the same size and hold the same type of data (values, text
labels) in the same order in both files.

If you cannot convert the other application's data, you may still be
able to import it into 1-2-3 if your other application can create an
ASCII file known as a *comma-delimited file.* Figure 16.3 illustrates
a comma-delimited file that would be compatible with the database
that was shown in Figure 16.1.

Notice that the fields in the comma-delimited file are in the same
order as the fields in the example 1-2-3 database. Each record is on a
single line. Each field's non-numeric data is enclosed within quotation marks. (Quotation marks are not required for numeric data—such
as the income amounts in the last field.) And finally, the fields are
separated by commas. Spaces can be added between the fields to
align them in columns and improve the readability of the file, but
they are not required.

As with other forms of data exchange, the order of fields in the
comma-delimited file must be the same as the order of fields in
the 1-2-3 database that is to receive it. Once you have created a
comma-delimited file with the proper structure, you can import it
into 1-2-3 by moving the cell pointer to where you want the new
data to reside and picking File from the menu bar, followed by
Import From and Numbers.

Enter the name of the comma-delimited file in the File **n**ame text
box in the File Import From Numbers dialog box or pick the file

```
"Art"    , "Finn"  , "765 Sagamore St." , "York"      , "PA" , "17402" , 85000
"Jane"   , "Lee"   , "163 N. 42nd St."  , "Milwaukee" , "WI" , "53209" , 30000
"John"   , "Hurst" , "4011 Peak Blvd."  , "Sudbury"   , "MA" , "01776" , 56000
"Ann"    , "Scott" , "2840 Plato Blvd." , "St. Paul"  , "MN" , "55107" , 72000
"Elaine" , "Duck"  , "105 State St."    , "Windsor"   , "VT" , "05089" , 61000
"John"   , "Saxon" , "462 SE 130th St." , "Belleview" , "FL" , "32620" , 97500
```

Figure 16.3: A comma-delimited file

name if it appears in the Files list box. Pick the OK button or press Enter to import the file.

Bear in mind that there must be sufficient memory available to hold the additional records you are importing. If 1-2-3 runs out of memory, it will abort the importing process and issue an "out of memory" error. If this happens, pick the OK button or press Esc, delete records as necessary to free up memory, edit the ASCII file to eliminate those records that were successfully imported, and resume the data exchange.

Manipulating a Database

In this step you will learn how to manipulate the database you have created. Basic database-manipulation techniques include filling cells with data, sorting the database, searching it for specific records, and extracting lists.

Filling a Range

Suppose you wanted to keep track of the database's original order of record entry. As you will see, when you sort a database, the previous order of entry is lost. However, you could add a column to the database that contained each record's original row number. Then you could sort on that column to return the database to its natural input order.

It would be tedious to input all those row numbers in a large database; fortunately, a special command sequence allows you to *fill* a range with a value that is incremented by a fixed amount.

You fill ranges with data by highlighting the desired range and then picking **Data** from the menu bar, followed by **Fill**.

1. First, create a new column to hold the original row numbers by moving the cell pointer to A3 in the example database and picking Worksheet followed by Insert. In the Worksheet Insert dialog box, indicate that you want to insert a Column, then pick the OK button or press Enter. This inserts a blank column at A.

2. Change the column width to 4 by picking Worksheet, followed by Column width, and when the dialog box appears, enter **4** in the Set width to: text box.

3. Enter the following label in A3:

   `Row

4. You now have a field named *Row.* Move the cell pointer to A5 and highlight the range A5..A19.

5. Pick **Data** followed by **Fill** or press Alt-DF. A dialog box appears.

6. Pick the **Start** text box and enter the current row number, **5**, as the starting value.

7. The **Step** text box should contain a default value of 1. If this is not the case, pick the box (if using the keyboard, press Alt-T) and enter **1**.

8. The **Stop** text box should contain the highest number required to fill the highlighted range. Since the example range is relatively small, you can leave it set for the current default, 8191. If you do decide to change it, it should be no lower than 19, the highest row number in the example range. Notice that having a stop number higher than what is required has no effect other than filling the range.

9. When the correct parameters are set, pick the **OK** button or press Enter. The program responds by filling the cells in the indicated range with data, incrementing the number in each cell as it proceeds throughout the range. When you are finished, your database should look like the one in Figure 17.1.

Sorting

You can manage your database more efficiently if it is sorted. You *sort* a database by arranging the records according to data in one or two selected *key fields.* The sort can be in either ascending (lowest-to-highest) or descending (highest-to-lowest) order. Any field can be used.

Before sorting your database, pick the **File Save** or **File Save As** command. This creates a backup in case something goes wrong.

If fields containing labels are used, the sort is alphabetical: Lower-case letters precede uppercase. For example, *b* follows *A*, but comes before *B*. Labels that start with numerals come before those that

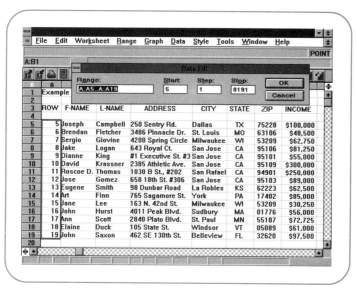

ROW	F-NAME	L-NAME	ADDRESS	CITY	STATE	ZIP	INCOME
5	Joseph	Campbell	250 Sentry Rd.	Dallas	TX	75228	$100,000
6	Brendan	Fletcher	3486 Pinnacle Dr.	St. Louis	MO	63106	$48,500
7	Sergio	Giovine	4200 Spring Circle	Milwaukee	WI	53209	$62,750
8	Jake	Logan	643 Royal Ct.	San Jose	CA	95106	$81,250
9	Dianne	King	#1 Executive St. #3	San Jose	CA	95101	$55,000
10	David	Krassner	2385 Athletic Ave.	San Jose	CA	95109	$300,000
11	Roscoe D.	Thomas	1030 B St., #202	San Rafael	CA	94901	$250,000
12	Jose	Gomez	658 18th St. #306	San Jose	CA	95103	$89,000
13	Eugene	Smith	98 Dunbar Road	La Robles	KS	62223	$62,500
14	Art	Finn	765 Sagamore St.	York	PA	17402	$85,000
15	Jane	Lee	163 N. 42nd St.	Milwaukee	WI	53209	$30,250
16	John	Hurst	4011 Peak Blvd.	Sudbury	MA	01776	$56,000
17	Ann	Scott	2840 Plato Blvd.	St. Paul	MN	55107	$72,725
18	Elaine	Duck	105 State St.	Windsor	VT	05089	$61,000
19	John	Saxon	462 SE 130th St.	Belleview	FL	32620	$97,500

Figure 17.1: A 1-2-3 database with a range filled in column A

start with alpha characters. When you sort fields that contain values, the sort is numeric.

To sort the example database in alphabetical order, do the following:

1. Highlight the data range. The data range should include all the fields in all the records you intend to sort. To sort the entire example database, highlight the range A5..H19.

2. Pick **Data** from the menu bar, followed by **Sort**. The Data Sort dialog box appears. Be sure that the highlighted range is indicated in the Data range: text box.

3. Now specify the key fields for the sort. Pick the **Primary** key: text box with the mouse pointer, or press Alt-P.

4. Enter the range of last names, C5..C19, using any of the methods you have learned previously for entering ranges of cells. If you have named this range, you may enter the range name in the text box.

5. Pick the Ascending multiple-choice button just below the primary-key range or press Alt-A.

6. Pick the Secondary key: text box with the mouse pointer or press Alt-S.

7. Enter the range of first names, B5..B19, or, if you have named the range, enter the range name.

8. Pick the Ascending multiple-choice button just below the secondary-key range, or press Alt-E.

9. When all parameters are correctly entered, pick the OK button or press Enter, and the highlighted records will be sorted. The time it takes to sort depends on the number of records in the database.

Mixed Sorts

You can sort on different data types and mix ascending and descending order. For example, suppose you want to sort the database by income, highest to lowest, and within the same income amount, alphabetically by name.

Use the INCOME range as your primary key field, and choose Descending sort order. Use the L-NAME range as your secondary key and choose Ascending sort order. This will produce the desired result.

Searching the Database

The **Data Query** command allows you to search a database for a particular record or set of records. The *query* operation requires an Input range, a Criteria range, and, if you are going to print the results of your search or extract them elsewhere, an Output range.

Input ranges

The input range is the complete range of records and fields you want to search. You can search all or part of your database. The criteria range is located in a separate area of the worksheet. It includes a row of field names to search and the data for which you are searching.

For example, suppose you want to find the records of all employees with incomes of $100,000 or greater.

1. To begin, set up your criteria range in the worksheet. Move the cell pointer to A21 and enter the search field name, **INCOME**. Be sure to type the field name exactly as it appears in the field name row, or use 1-2-3's **Edit Quick Copy** command to copy it.

2. Move the cell pointer down one cell to A22 and enter the following label:

   `>=100000`

   Use standard 1-2-3 mathematical operators in your criteria ranges to create search mechanisms. The formula you just typed in will be understood by 1-2-3 to mean "Any value that is greater than or equal to 100,000."

3. Now you are ready to begin the search. Move the cell pointer to cell A3, which is in the row containing the field names, and highlight the range A3..H19.

4. Pick **Data** from the menu bar, followed by **Query**.

5. Since you would like to search the entire example database, check the **Input range:** text box (or press Alt-I) and confirm that it indicates the range A3 through H19. Notice that this range includes the row containing the field names. You must include the field name row whenever you search a 1-2-3 database.

6. Pick the **Criteria range:** text box.

7. Move the cell pointer to cell A21 and highlight the range A21 to A22.

8. To highlight all the records that match your criteria, invoke the **Find** option from the Data Query menu. Lotus 1-2-3 will begin by highlighting the first record it finds that matches your criteria. Press the ↓ key to find the next record, and continue pressing the ↓ key until the last matching record is found. To return to the Data Query menu, press Esc.

Extracting a Range

You can instruct 1-2-3 to extract all the records that match a given set of criteria and then copy them to a new area of the worksheet. This operation is similar to the search operation you just learned. As before, you must indicate input and criteria ranges, but in addition, you must specify an *output range*.

Output ranges

To specify an output range, copy the field names that you would like to list to a blank area of the worksheet. They should all be in the same row. Figure 17.2 shows an output range consisting of the same field names as the example database. In actual practice, you need not specify all the field names, nor do you have to include them in the same order as in the original database.

It is best not to have any additional data below the output range, because records will be extracted and copied to this location, overwriting any data that is there.

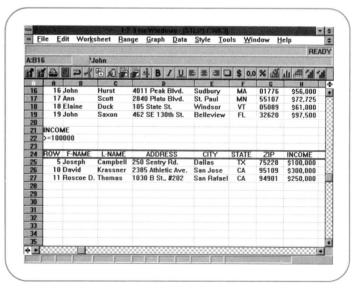

Figure 17.2: Output range with data matching the criteria range

After you list the output field names, pick **D**ata from the menu bar, followed by **Q**uery. In the Data Query dialog box, check that the input range is A3..H19, and the criteria range is A21..A22, as before.

Next, Pick the **O**utput range text box or press Alt-O. When the range in the box is highlighted, enter the range A24..H24, which is the row containing the copied field names, or highlight that range using the mouse pointer. When all parameters have been set, pick the **E**xtract button, or press Alt-E. All records matching the criteria will be copied below the output range.

When you create more complicated searches, test the logic of your criteria ranges on a small input range whose results can be easily verified. Then perform the search on the full input range. By testing first on a small sample, you can easily spot and rectify problems in your criteria ranges.

Step 18

Defining Macros

The ability to create macros is one of 1-2-3's most powerful features. A *macro* is a recording of keystrokes. When you play back the recording, 1-2-3 accepts the keystrokes just as if you had entered them from the keyboard. Macros save time and increase productivity by eliminating repetitive command entry, executing commands faster, and preventing the errors that occur during manual command entry.

Macros can become quite complicated, incorporating such standard computer programming constructs as variables, branching, and controlled looping. While macro writing is not a full-fledged programming language, many clever users and developers have created entire applications based on 1-2-3 macros. This step will teach you the basics. When you have completed this step, you will have a good foundation for building simple, useful macros and learning more about 1-2-3's advanced macro capabilities.

Defining Macros

There are three steps to creating and using a macro: recording it, naming it, and executing it. These steps are described in detail in the following sections.

Recording Keystrokes

You can record keystrokes by entering them as a label in a cell (or a range of cells in a column). The command sequence is called a *macro label;* the starting cell of the range is called the *macro cell.* All 1-2-3 keystrokes can be expressed in macros. Alphanumeric and punctuation keys are entered literally. Other special keys, such as the arrow keys or function keys, are entered using special symbols. You can find these symbols in your 1-2-3 documentation.

For example, suppose you wanted to create a macro that would fill a row with a horizontal line. You have already seen the manual technique for doing this in previous steps. Following is a macro label that represents the same series of keystrokes. To enter this macro, move the cell pointer to an empty cell below and to the right of the data in your worksheet, and enter the exact series of characters that you see here:

```
'\-~{paneloff}{alt}ec{r}{abs}{?}~{alt}ep{panelon}
```

This macro may at first appear to be gibberish, but if you break it down, keystroke by keystroke, its meaning becomes clear:

- The apostrophe (') is the label format code for a left-justified label. This character is ignored when the macro is executed. Its purpose is to signal that what follows is a label, not a formula or value.

- The backward slash (\) and the hyphen (-) are the keystrokes to enter a repeating-hyphen label in a cell.

- The tilde (~) represents the Enter key, which is what you would press now if you were manually entering the repeating-hyphen label from the keyboard.

- *{paneloff}* temporarily turns off display of the control panel, so it does not flash during the execution of the macro.

- *{alt}ec* represents the keystrokes required to invoke 1-2-3's **E**dit **C**opy command.

- *{r}* indicates one press of the → key. This moves the cell pointer one cell to the right.

- *{abs}{?}~* anchors the cell pointer and returns control of the worksheet to you. At this point, you can move the cell pointer and highlight any range of cells you like. After you highlight the range, press Enter to indicate the end of your input, and 1-2-3 will continue with the macro. By pausing for input here, the macro stays flexible; when you execute it, you can draw lines of any length. Notice that a tilde follows this sequence. This tilde instructs 1-2-3 to enter the highlighted range.

- *{alt}ep* represents the keystrokes required to invoke 1-2-3's **Edit P**aste command. The line in the first cell is now copied into the range.

- *{panelon}* redisplays changes in the control panel.

Notice that when you press the Enter key at the end of your input, that keypress is not considered part of the macro's keystroke sequence; it only signals the end of your input.

After you have entered the keystrokes into a cell, you must name the macro cell. Do this using the same command sequence you used to name ranges: pick **R**ange from the menu bar, followed by **N**ame, followed by **C**reate. The Range Name Create dialog box appears.

Macro names often consist of a backslash character (\) followed by a letter or a single digit. If possible, try to use a letter that will remind you of the macro's function, then you can run the macro by holding down the Ctrl key and pressing the character key.

Macro names are mnemonic

Macro names may also follow 1-2-3's rules for naming any range of cells; this is, you can use any combination of up to fifteen characters. When you give a macro a long name, you can start it by pressing Alt-F3 (or by picking **T**ools from the menu bar, followed by **M**acro and **R**un) and then selecting the macro from the displayed list of range names.

Enter the name of the macro in the **R**ange name: text box. For example, to name the macro you just created, specify the name:

\H

and click the OK button. The backslash is required, as it signals to 1-2-3 that the label in the highlighted cell is a macro. The letter *H* was chosen to stand for *Horizontal line.*

Invoking the Macro

To play back the macro you have just defined, move the cell pointer to a cell in an empty row, hold down the Ctrl key, and press **H**. Instantly, the cell fills with a line, and the cell pointer moves to the right one cell. You must now enter a range. Using the → key, move the cell pointer further to the right until an acceptable range is highlighted and press Enter. A line then fills the highlighted range.

As you can see, this is a lot more convenient than manually drawing the line and invoking the Edit Copy and Paste commands throughout the worksheet.

Macro Rules

There are a few rules that govern macros:

- Macro keystrokes can be recorded in a single cell or a range of cells. You can enter up to 512 characters per cell.

- Macros are not case-sensitive; all keystrokes are treated as uppercase.

- Macros can be entered in a range of cells occupying a single column. You may split the sequence of macro keystrokes at any point to promote readability. Figure 18.1 shows the example macro split into a series of labels.

- When a macro occupies a range of cells, only the first cell need be named. The program will attempt to execute the keystrokes found in the cells below the named cell until an empty cell is encountered.

- If you enter more than one macro in a worksheet, each must have a unique name.

- By default, a macro named \0 (backslash-zero) is executed automatically when a worksheet is first loaded. You can disable and re-enable this feature using the Tools User Setup command.

- Macros can be stored in separate worksheets and brought into other worksheets using the File Combine From

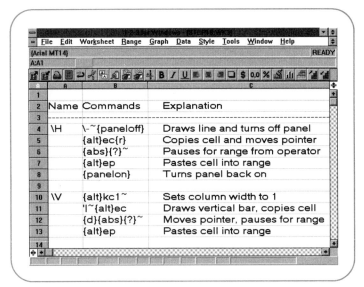

Figure 18.1: Example macros in a worksheet, with documentation

command. When you combine a worksheet containing a macro, use the Range Name Create command to rename the macro's cells in the current worksheet.

Documenting Macros

As you can see from the above example, the meaning of even a relatively simple macro is not immediately obvious. Figure 18.1 illustrates a standard method for documenting macros. The macro name is entered as a label in the cell to the left of the macro's starting cell, and a brief explanation is entered in a cell to its right. Documenting helps you keep track of what your macros do.

Debugging Macros

When you're developing a macro, first go through the keystrokes at the keyboard, noting them on a piece of paper. Then, when you have written down the sequence, copy it into the worksheet.

*Macros
do not
recognize
errors*

Some of your macros may not execute perfectly the first time. A macro does not evaluate keystrokes for correctness; it attempts to execute whatever keystrokes the macro label contains, whether right or wrong. If you make a mistake in entering the keystrokes, the macro will probably malfunction.

Typos and misspellings are common macro errors, as is neglecting the tildes that represent Enter keystrokes. Look for these errors first if you are having trouble making a macro work.

When a macro encounters a keystroke it cannot process, it stops functioning and puts 1-2-3 into ERROR mode. You can return to READY mode by pressing Esc; depending on the point at which the macro malfunctioned, you may have to press Esc several times. You can interrupt a macro during its processing by pressing Ctrl-Break and Esc. If a macro does not perform as expected, use 1-2-3's EDIT mode (function key F2) to revise the macro, just as you would any label.

Because macros execute quickly, it may not be easy to discern exactly where a problem occurs. You can slow down a macro by placing 1-2-3 in STEP mode:

1. Invoke Step mode by pressing Alt-F2.

2. Start the macro.

3. Go to each successive keystroke in the macro by pressing the spacebar or arrow keys.

4. Finish the macro.

5. Turn off step mode by pressing F2 again.

This lets you slowly progress through a macro, noting the results of each keystroke, and isolate the source of the problem.

To use the menus to place 1-2-3 in STEP mode, pick **Tools** from the menu bar, followed by **Macro**, followed by **Debug**. Pick **Single Step** from the Tools Macro Debug dialog box, then pick the **OK** button or press Enter. Notice that the STEP indicator lights up in the status bar at the bottom of the window. To exit STEP mode, pick the same series of commands and toggle off Single Step.

Creating Macros
with the Windows Clipboard

Lotus 1-2-3 keeps track of your command and keystroke sequences, storing a *keystroke transcript* as you work with your spreadsheets. You can extract portions of this transcript and place them in cells to become macros.

To see the transcript, pick Tools from the menu bar, followed by Macro, followed by Show transcript. You will see a *Transcript window*, which includes a macro-style representation of the commands you have entered.

You can use standard Windows editing commands to edit the transcript or copy portions of it to the Windows clipboard. After you have copied a portion of the transcript to the clipboard, close the Transcript window, return to the worksheet, and highlight a cell. Pick Edit from the menu bar, followed by Paste, and the saved keystrokes will be pasted into the highlighted cell. In some cases, the transcript will occupy other cells below the highlighted one.

After you move the keystroke transcript, you can continue to edit it, if necessary. Don't forget to name it, with the Range Name Create command, as described earlier.

The program's keystroke-recording feature works for most keystrokes, but you cannot use this feature to include the symbol that pauses the macro for user input. If you need to include this symbol ({?}), you must edit the transcript.

Lotus 1-2-3 includes special features that allow you to format your printed output in ways not available with ordinary text-based worksheets. By combining your worksheet with special graphics-based page-formatting commands, you can produce results previously available only with expensive desktop-publishing software.

Changing Your Text's Fonts and Appearance

To change the size and appearance of your worksheet's text, highlight the cells containing the text you would like to change, then pick Style from the menu bar, followed by Font. A dialog box shows you a list of eight currently available fonts.

If the desired font is not on the list, pick the Replace button. Another dialog box will appear, showing the currently available fonts and a second list of fonts from which you may choose a replacement.

First, highlight a font that you don't need in the Current font list using the mouse pointer or arrow keys, followed by Enter. Then highlight a font type in the Available font list, and a point size in the Size list. When the correct fonts are highlighted, pick the Replace button.

If you would like the new current fonts to become the default font list, pick the Update button. You can also save any given font list as a named file. To do this, pick the Save button. You will then be prompted to provide a name for the font list. Font list files have the extension .AF3. Enter the font-list name using the technique you learned when saving worksheet files. When you are finished replacing fonts, pick the OK button or press Enter.

Changing a Font

For example, suppose you wanted to change the title in row A of the Income/Expense Statement from its current font to a bolder one.

Press the Home key to move the cell pointer to A1, and pick Style Font. When the Style Font dialog box appears, pick ArialMT 14 from the font list, or a similar font of your choosing. Pick the OK button or press enter, and 1-2-3 changes the text in cell A1.

To center the header in the worksheet, highlight the top row, then pick Style from the menu bar, followed by Alignment. The program displays the Style Alignment dialog box. Pick Center from the multiple-choice list and activate the *Align over columns* toggle switch. Pick the OK button or press Enter after making your selections.

You can similarly reformat ranges of cells. For example, try formatting the rest of the worksheet to TimesNewRomanPS 10 point.

Changing Font Appearance

You can add certain features to the fonts that you select, such as boldface, italics, or underlining. For example, suppose you wanted to add boldface to the month headings in row 3 of the example worksheet.

Move the cell pointer to B3 and highlight the range B3 to H3. Pick Style Font, and activate the Bold toggle switch in the Style Font dialog box. Pick the OK button or press Enter, and the text is made boldface.

You can underline the labels in a highlighted range of cells by activating the Underline toggle switch in the same dialog box. You have a choice of three underlining styles. Pick the button to the right of the current underline style and a second box appears, allowing you to scroll through to your choice of underlining styles: Single, Double, or Wide.

Outlining a Range

Furthermore, you can add lines to your worksheet to set off text and improve its appearance. To draw lines in your worksheet, pick Style from the menu bar, followed by Border. A dialog box appears, offering you a choice of one of the following types of lines:

All edges	Outlines each cell in a range
Top	Draws a horizontal line on top of a range
Bottom	Draws a horizontal line beneath a range
Left	Draws a vertical line to the left of a range
Right	Draws a vertical line to the right of a range
Outline	Draws a box around a range
Drop Shadow	Adds a shadow effect to a line or box

For example, suppose you wanted to highlight the first and second quarter in the Income Expense Statement. Highlight the range B3 through D22, then pick Style Border, select Outline, and pick the OK button. Do the same thing with the range E3 through G22.

Changing Row Size

Unlike a text-based worksheet, 1-2-3 for Windows gives you the ability to change the size of rows to accommodate any size of text font. By default, 1-2-3 handles this process automatically, but you can manually change the height of individual rows if you so desire.

To change the size of rows, first highlight a cell (or range of cells) in the rows you want to change. Then pick Worksheet from the menu bar, followed by Row Height. When the dialog box appears, enter the new height in points. Valid point sizes range from 1 to 255.

Use discretion when deciding upon a point size. A point size that is too small will mask a portion of the text, while one that is too large will waste space.

Alternatively, you can indicate the row sizes dynamically. To do this, move the pointer to the border line below the row number. When you do this, the pointer icon changes to a double arrow. Now hold the pick button down as you move the pointer up or down. A horizontal line appears on the worksheet, moving as you move the pointer. This line indicates the new height of the row. When the line is in the correct position, release the pick button, and the row height is changed.

Figure 19.1 illustrates how a reformatted worksheet might look. Notice that some changes have been made to the row and column sizes to accommodate the text on one screen. Try making similar changes to your example worksheet, using the commands you have learned so far.

Importing Graphs

The ability to combine graphs and text in the printed worksheet is an important feature of 1-2-3 for Windows. You may combine any graph that you have stored in the worksheet.

For example, suppose you wanted to place the line graph that you created in Steps 14 and 15 below the text in the example worksheet. Assume that you have named the graph GRAPH2, and that the named graph is part of the current file. If you have not created or

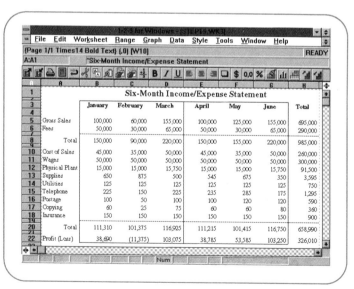

Figure 19.1: The example worksheet with text formatting added

named such a graph, refer back to Steps 14 and 15 for details on creating it.

Move the cell pointer to cell B25 and highlight the range B25 through G42. Pick Graph from the menu bar, followed by Add to Sheet. Select the line graph from the list of named graphs in the dialog box.

This feature allows you to import the graph into an exact area of the worksheet. Graphs will be distorted to accommodate the range you highlight, so it is usually best to pick a range that reflects the actual dimensions of the graph.

The file Preview feature is especially useful when adding graphs to worksheets, as this feature will display each page of the currently configured output on the screen, allowing you to double-check its layout and appearance before actually printing it. To preview the current example worksheet, pick File from the menu bar, followed by Preview. Figure 19.2 illustrates a screen preview of the example worksheet.

Preview saves printing time

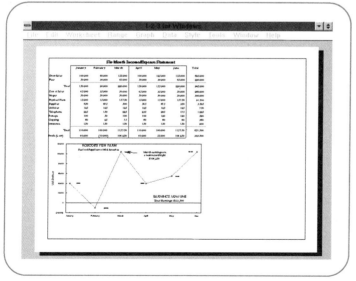

Figure 19.2: A preview of the example worksheet's printed output.

Solver is a feature of 1-2-3 for Windows that allows you to analyze worksheets and determine different possible solutions to *what-if* problems. Using solver, you can select cells with variable values, set up specific conditions for solving problems, and determine the best possible solution.

For example, suppose you were using the example Income/Expense worksheet shown in Figure 20.1, and you wanted to determine the amount of gross sales for the month of June required to make a $200,000 profit under the following conditions:

1.   Income from fees does not exceed fifty percent of gross sales.

2.   Wages do not exceed the cost of sales.

Solver could find this gross sales figure for you. Using the example worksheet, enter the figures for June's income and expenses in Column G, as shown in Figure 20.1. Be sure to enter formulas in cells G8 (Total), G15 (Total), and G17 (Profit/Loss) if they don't contain formulas already. (The titles have been locked vertically for the sake of readability.)

To set up the conditions for solving the problem, move the cell pointer to cell I3 and enter the following formula:

    +G17>=200000

This formula indicates that the value in cell G17, Profit, must be greater than or equal to $200,000. Move the cell pointer to cell I4 and enter:

    +G12<=G11

This formula indicates that the value in cell G12, Wages, must be less than or equal to the value in cell G11, Cost of Sales. Move the cell pointer to cell I5 and enter

    +G6<=G5*0.5

This formula means that the value in cell G6, Fees, must be less than or equal to one-half the value in cell G5, Gross Sales.

The formulas you have entered are logical formulas. This means that they return either 1, meaning that the condition is true, or 0, meaning that the condition is false. Solver uses these formulas as the basis for selecting the optimum set of numbers in column G that will make all these conditions evaluate as true.

The next step is to invoke the Solver and set up the problem. To do this, you must tell 1-2-3 to use the logical formulas you have just entered, and indicate which cells contain numbers to be changed.

1. Pick Tools from the menu bar, followed by Solver. The Solver Definition dialog box appears, which you use to set up the problem.

2. Enter the range G5 through G13 in the first text box, Adjustable cells. Solver will change the values in these cells when it solves the problem.

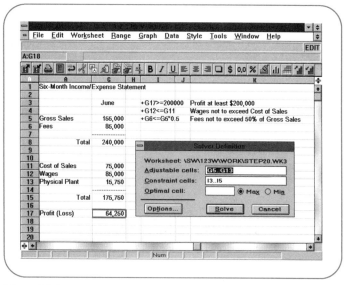

Figure 20.1: Example worksheet for use with 1-2-3 Solver

3. Enter the range I3 through I5 in the next text box, Constraint cells. These cells contain the formulas that define the problem.

The last text box, Optimal cell, is not used in this example. In more complicated problems involving several possible answers, you can use this text box to enter a cell that 1-2-3 uses to display the answer that best solves the problem. In this example, leave it blank.

When you have entered the parameters for the problem, pick the Solve button. First, a dialog box will pop up, giving you a status report of the Search For solutions. Then 1-2-3 will display the answer to the problem, as illustrated in Figure 20.2.

By default, Solver attempts to find up to ten possible answers for a problem. In this example, it has found only one, and has changed the values in column G. The Solver Answer dialog box indicates which answer is being displayed. If you would like to compare the displayed answer to the original values in the worksheet, pick the

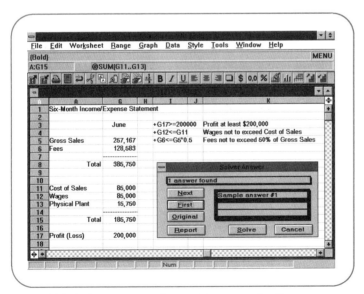

Figure 20.2: Solver computes the requisite gross sales figure.

Original button. To see each possible answer in turn, pick the Next button. To see the first answer found, pick the First button.

In problems that have more than ten possible answers, pick the Solve button to solve for more answers than are currently given.

Pick the Report button to produce various reports containing information on how Solver arrived at its solutions. When you pick this button, a dialog box appears offering you a choice of the various kinds of reports:

- *Answer table* lists all answers found for the problem. Since the report is saved as a worksheet file, it is possible to use this report to create a graph of Solver answers.

- *Cells used* lists the cells used to solve the problem, along with information about each cell's contents. Use this report to analyze the way you set up the problem to be solved.

- *How solved* shows the method used to arrive at the answers to the problem. This is a good overall report of cells and formulas and will help you evaluate the validity of the Solver's answers.

- *What-if limits* indicates the range of values in the adjustable cells that fulfill the conditions of the problem. This report will help you determine the extent to which you can adjust values in variable cells and still arrive at a valid answer to the problem.

- *Differences* compares answers that differ by an amount that you specify, when the problem has more than one solution. This report can help you choose which answer is the best one, given your considerations.

- *Unused constraints* lists any logical formulas that were not required to solve the problem. Use this report to eliminate unneeded formulas, thus setting up the most efficient problem for the Solver to process.

- *Inconsistent constraints* shows which formulas evaluate to false in the currently displayed solution to the problem.

Use this report to find the formulas that prevented Solver from finding an answer to your problem.

Saving Solver Answers

To save the answers that solver finds, display the answer you want to save in the worksheet file, then close the Solver dialog box by picking Close from its control menu or pressing Esc. Use **File Save** or **File Save As** to save the worksheet.

If you want to save a list of all the answers Solver has found, pick the **Report** button in the Solver dialog box, followed by **Answer** table. Close the Solver dialog box and pick the window containing the report, making it current. Use **File Save** or **File Save As** to save the report to a worksheet file.

Solver problems can become quite complex, including large ranges of variable value cells and long lists of logical formulas. The number of cells and formulas involved is limited by the amount of memory you have available. If you receive an out-of-memory message when running Solver, you must attempt to simplify the problem.

Cells that contain functions usually take more time and memory to solve. Include cells with these functions only when necessary. Do not include cells with functions that take string arguments, string-parsing functions, database functions, date functions, or time functions. Do not use functions in cells that contain Solver's logical-formula parameters, or in the optimum-value cell.

Index

Selections from The SYBEX Library

SPREADSHEETS AND INTEGRATED SOFTWARE

1-2-3 for Scientists and Engineers
William J. Orvis
371pp. Ref. 733-9
This up-to-date edition offers fast, elegant solutions to common problems in science and engineering. Complete, carefully explained techniques for plotting, curve fitting, statistics, derivatives, integrals and differentials, solving systems of equations, and more; plus useful Lotus add-ins.

The ABC's of 1-2-3 (Second Edition)
Chris Gilbert
Laurie Williams
245pp. Ref. 355-4
Online Today recommends it as "an easy and comfortable way to get started with the program." An essential tutorial for novices, it will remain on your desk as a valuable source of ongoing reference and support. For Release 2.

The ABC's of 1-2-3 Release 2.2
Chris Gilbert
Laurie Williams
340pp. Ref. 623-5
New Lotus 1-2-3 users delight in this book's step-by-step approach to building trouble-free spreadsheets, displaying graphs, and efficiently building databases. The authors cover the ins and outs of the latest version including easier calculations, file linking, and better graphic presentation.

The ABC's of 1-2-3 Release 2.3
Chris Gilbert
Laurie Williams
350pp. Ref. 837-8

Computer Currents called it "one of the best tutorials available." This new edition provides easy-to-follow, hands-on lessons tailored specifically for computer and spreadsheet newcomers—or for anyone seeking a quick and easy guide to the basics. Covers everything from switching on the computer to charts, functions, macros, and important new features.

The ABC's of 1-2-3 Release 3
Judd Robbins
290pp. Ref. 519-0
The ideal book for beginners who are new to Lotus or new to Release 3. This step-by-step approach to the 1-2-3 spreadsheet software gets the reader up and running with spreadsheet, database, graphics, and macro functions.

The ABC's of Excel on the IBM PC
Douglas Hergert
326pp. Ref. 567-0
This book is a brisk and friendly introduction to the most important features of Microsoft Excel for PC's. This beginner's book discusses worksheets, charts, database operations, and macros, all with hands-on examples. Written for all versions through Version 2.

The ABC's of Quattro Pro 3
Alan Simpson
Douglas Wolf
338pp. Ref. 836-6
This popular beginner's tutorial on Quattro Pro 2 shows first-time computer and spreadsheet users the essentials of electronic number-crunching. Topics range from business spreadsheet design to error-free formulas, presentation slide shows, the database, macros, more.

The Complete Lotus 1-2-3 Release 2.2 Handbook
Greg Harvey

750pp. Ref. 625-1
This comprehensive handbook discusses every 1-2-3 operation with clear instructions and practical tips. This volume especially emphasizes the new improved graphics, high-speed recalculation techniques, and spreadsheet linking available with Release 2.2.

The Complete Lotus 1-2-3 Release 3 Handbook
Greg Harvey
700pp. Ref. 600-6
Everything you ever wanted to know about 1-2-3 is in this definitive handbook. As a Release 3 guide, it features the design and use of 3D worksheets, and improved graphics, along with using Lotus under DOS or OS/2. Problems, exercises, and helpful insights are included.

Lotus 1-2-3 2.2 On-Line Advisor Version 1.1
SYBAR, Software Division of SYBEX, Inc.
Ref. 935-8
Need Help fast? With a touch of a key, the Advisor pops up right on top of your Lotus 1-2-3 program to answer your spreadsheet questions. With over 4000 index citations and 1600 pre-linked cross-references, help has never been so easy to find. Just start typing your topic and the Lotus 1-2-3 Advisor does all the look-up for you. Covers versions 2.01 and 2.2. Software package comes with 3½" and 5¼" disks. System Requirements: IBM compatible with DOS 2.0 or higher, runs with Windows 3.0, uses 90K of RAM.

Lotus 1-2-3 Desktop Companion SYBEX Ready Reference Series
Greg Harvey
976pp. Ref. 501-8
A full-time consultant, right on your desk. Hundreds of self-contained entries cover every 1-2-3 feature, organized by topic, indexed and cross-referenced, and supplemented by tips, macros and working examples. For Release 2.

Lotus 1-2-3 Instant Reference Release 2.2 SYBEX Prompter Series
Greg Harvey
Kay Yarborough Nelson
254pp. Ref. 635-9
The reader gets quick and easy access to any operation in 1-2-3 Version 2.2 in this handy pocket-sized encyclopedia. Organized by menu function, each command and function has a summary description, the exact key sequence, and a discussion of the options.

Lotus 1-2-3 Tips and Tricks (2nd edition)
Gene Weisskopf
425pp. Ref. 668-5
This outstanding collection of tips, shortcuts and cautions for longtime Lotus users is in an expanded new edition covering Release 2.2. Topics include macros, range names, spreadsheet design, hardware and operating system tips, data analysis, printing, data interchange, applications development, and more.

Mastering 1-2-3 (Second Edition)
Carolyn Jorgensen
702pp. Ref. 528-X
Get the most from 1-2-3 Release 2.01 with this step-by-step guide emphasizing advanced features and practical uses. Topics include data sharing, macros, spreadsheet security, expanded memory, and graphics enhancements.

Mastering 1-2-3 Release 3
Carolyn Jorgensen
682pp. Ref. 517-4
For new Release 3 and experienced Release 2 users, "Mastering" starts with a basic spreadsheet, then introduces spreadsheet and database commands, functions, and macros, and then tells how to analyze 3D spreadsheets and make high-impact reports and graphs. Lotus add-ons are discussed and Fast Tracks are included.

Mastering Enable/OA
Christopher Van Buren
Robert Bixby
540pp. Ref 637-5
This is a structured, hands-on guide to integrated business computing, for users who want to achieve productivity in the shortest possible time. Separate in-depth sections cover word processing, spreadsheets, databases, telecommunications, task integration and macros.

Mastering Excel on the IBM PC
Carl Townsend
628pp. Ref. 403-8
A complete Excel handbook with step-by-step tutorials, sample applications and an extensive reference section. Topics include worksheet fundamentals, formulas and windows, graphics, database techniques, special features, macros and more.

Mastering Excel 3 for Windows
Carl Townsend
625pp. Ref. 643-X
A new edition of SYBEX's highly praised guide to the Excel super spreadsheet, under Windows 3.0. Includes full coverage of new features; dozens of tips and examples; in-depth treatment of specialized topics, including presentation graphics and macros; and sample applications for inventory control, financial management, trend analysis, and more.

Mastering Framework III
Douglas Hergert
Jonathan Kamin
613pp. Ref. 513-1
Thorough, hands-on treatment of the latest Framework release. An outstanding introduction to integrated software applications, with examples for outlining, spreadsheets, word processing, databases, and more; plus an introduction to FRED programming.

Mastering Freelance Plus
Donald Richard Read
411pp. Ref. 701-0
A detailed guide to high-powered graphing and charting with Freelance Plus. Part I is a practical overview of the software.

Part II offers concise tutorials on creating specific chart types. Part III covers drawing functions in depth. Part IV shows how to organize and generate output, including printing and on-screen shows.

Mastering Quattro Pro 2
Gene Weisskopf
575pp, Ref. 792-4
This hands-on guide and reference takes readers from basic spreadsheets to creating three-dimensional graphs, spreadsheet databases, macros and advanced data analysis. Also covers Paradox Access and translating Lotus 1-2-3 2.2 work sheets. A great tutorial for beginning and intermediate users, this book also serves as a reference for users at all levels.

Mastering Quattro Pro 3
Gene Weisskopf
618pp. Ref. 841-6
A complete hands-on guide and on-the-job reference, offering practical tutorials on the basics; up-to-date treatment of advanced capabilities; highlighted coverage of new software features, and expert advice from author Gene Weisskopf, a seasoned spreadsheet specialist.

Mastering Smartware II
Jonathan Paul Bacon
634pp. Ref. 651-0
An easy-to-read, self-paced introduction to a powerful program. This book offers separate treatment of word processing, data file management, spreadsheets, and communications, with special sections on data integration between modules. Concrete examples from business are used throughout.

Mastering SuperCalc5
Greg Harvey
Mary Beth Andrasak
500pp. Ref. 624-3
This book offers a complete and unintimidating guided tour through each feature. With step-by-step lessons, readers learn about the full capabilities of spreadsheet, graphics, and data management functions. Multiple spreadsheets, linked spreadsheets, 3D graphics, and macros are also discussed.